K.R. DANIELS

The New Manager's Playbook

First-Time Managers Who Want to Lead with Confidence on Day One (Not Just Survive)

ASCENDA
PRESS

First edition

ISBN (paperback): 979-8-9993993-1-1
ISBN (hardcover): 979-8-9993993-2-8

This book was professionally typeset on Reedsy.
Find out more at reedsy.com

This book is dedicated to my wife, daughters, furry kids, and you, the new manager. I, too, was once a new manager.

"The only person you are destined to become is the person you decide to be."

Ralph Waldo Emerson

Contents

Introduction

Stepping into your first management role can feel like being handed a map in a foreign language—and expected to lead others through unfamiliar terrain. Maybe you've spent the night before your first team meeting wide awake, replaying every possible question your team might ask or worrying if they'll notice that twinge of doubt you keep hidden. If you've ever found yourself wondering, "Who let me do this?" or dodging eye contact with your old peers who now report to you, you're not alone.

The Hidden Reality of New Management

The statistics tell a sobering story: 87% of new managers feel unprepared for their role, and nearly 60% struggle with the transition for six months or longer. Yet most organizations provide less than 40 hours of management training in the first year—barely enough time to scratch the surface of what effective leadership truly requires.

The truth is that management is one of the few professions where excellence in your previous role—whether as an engineer, salesperson, teacher, or nurse—bears little resemblance to what you'll need for success in your new position. It's like being promoted from playing violin beautifully to conducting an entire orchestra. The skills that got you here won't be enough to take you forward.

This gap between expectation and reality creates what researchers call "the new manager transition crisis"—a period where capable professionals suddenly feel incompetent, overwhelmed, and isolated. You might excel at your technical work but struggle with giving feedback. You might have great ideas but find it difficult to motivate others to implement them. You might

1

care deeply about your team's success but lack the frameworks to translate that caring into effective leadership.

Why Most Management Advice Misses the Mark

Traditional management training focuses heavily on processes, policies, and procedures—the mechanics of management. While these elements matter, they miss the most challenging aspects of leadership: navigating human emotions, building trust across diverse personalities, making decisions with incomplete information, and maintaining your own confidence while supporting others through uncertainty.

Most management books offer generic advice that sounds reasonable in theory but falls apart when faced with real-world complexity. They tell you to "have difficult conversations" without acknowledging the knot in your stomach when you imagine actually doing it. They suggest "building psychological safety" without explaining how to create that environment when you're still figuring out your own role.

This book takes a different approach. Instead of academic theories, you'll find practical frameworks tested in real management situations. Rather than generic case studies, you'll read about managers that I worked with who look like you, sound like you, work in industries like yours, and face challenges similar to yours.

What Makes This Book Different

Real-World Application Focus: Every framework includes specific scripts, templates, and step-by-step guidance you can use immediately. You won't need to translate abstract concepts into actionable behaviors—that work is already done for you.

Industry and Cultural Diversity: The examples and case studies span healthcare, technology, manufacturing, education, nonprofit organizations, and service industries. You'll see managers of different ages, backgrounds, and experience levels navigating challenges relevant to your context.

Emotional Intelligence Integration: Management isn't just about systems and processes—it's fundamentally about human relationships. This book addresses the emotional aspects of leadership that other resources often overlook or minimize.

Progressive Skill Building: Each chapter builds on previous concepts while introducing new capabilities. You'll develop a comprehensive management toolkit that grows more sophisticated as your experience expands.

Practical Toolkit Integration: Rather than scattered checklists, you'll find a comprehensive Manager's Toolkit Appendix with assessment tools, conversation templates, and implementation guides you can reference throughout your career.

Your Journey Through This Book

The book is structured to mirror your natural development as a manager, starting with the internal work of understanding your new role and building personal effectiveness, then expanding to team leadership and organizational impact.

Part 1: Personal Foundation (Chapters 1-4) addresses the emotional and psychological aspects of your transition, helping you build self-awareness, define your leadership philosophy, and create a compelling vision that motivates others.

Part 2: Core Management Skills (Chapters 5-8) covers the fundamental interpersonal capabilities every manager needs: building trust, communicating effectively, hiring and developing talent, and creating inclusive team cultures.

Part 3: Advanced Leadership Capabilities (Chapters 9-12) explores complex challenges like managing remote teams, navigating conflict, thinking strategically, and leading through crisis.

Part 4: Future-Focused Leadership (Chapters 13-14) prepares you for evolving leadership demands and long-term career growth.

In the pages to follow, you will find real-world case studies, practical frameworks, reflection exercises, and specific action steps. The progression is intentional: early chapters focus on self-management and basic relationship building, middle chapters tackle day-to-day management challenges, and later chapters prepare you for strategic leadership and long-term impact.

Throughout the journey, real-world scenarios and case studies will illustrate how these principles are applied in practice. You'll read about managers who successfully navigated team conflicts, led through organizational changes, built inclusive cultures, and recovered from significant mistakes. These stories aren't meant to provide templates to copy but to show how thoughtful leaders adapt principles to their unique circumstances.

How to Get the Most from This Experience

Don't just read—pause to reflect, jot down answers to journal prompts, and try out the scripts or frameworks. Growth comes from noticing your progress, getting curious about your reactions, and experimenting with small changes. The difference between managers who struggle and those who thrive often comes down to their willingness to practice deliberately and reflect honestly on results.

Make use of the Manager's Toolkit Appendix, chapter challenges, and reflection exercises. Take these templates and tweak them until they fit you and your team. This book is your mentor-in-print, nudging you toward bolder actions and deeper self-understanding, one chapter at a time. The frameworks are starting points, not rigid rules; adapt them to your industry, team size, organizational culture, and personal style.

Consider keeping a management journal as you read, tracking your experiments with new approaches and reflecting on what works in your specific context. Note which tools feel natural and which require more practice. Pay attention to your team's responses to changes in your leadership style.

I know you're busy. That's why I've kept advice sharp, direct, and free from motivational fluff. Every lesson offers concrete takeaways you can use immediately—no expert-speak or management jargon to decode. Whether you're squeezing in ten minutes between meetings or tackling a full chapter over coffee, you'll find clarity, not complexity.

The Journey Ahead

The journey of becoming a manager is also a journey of personal growth. You'll discover strengths you didn't know you had and confront weaknesses you'd rather ignore. You'll be forced to clarify your values when they're tested by difficult decisions. You'll learn to manage not just other people's performance but also their emotions, aspirations, and professional development. This growth can be uncomfortable, but it's also profoundly rewarding.

Remember that every expert was once a beginner. The managers you most admire struggled with many of the same challenges you're facing now. They learned through experience, mistakes, feedback, and reflection—the same process you're beginning. Your willingness to invest in developing your leadership skills already distinguishes you from managers who assume they can figure it out through trial and error alone.

Your Commitment to Growth

So turn the page, take a breath, and commit to this journey. With each insight, tool, and experiment, you're building the foundation for the kind of leader you—and your team—will be proud of. The path ahead may be challenging, but it's also filled with opportunities to make a positive difference in people's lives and careers.

Your commitment to reading this book signals something important: you care enough about your team's success and well-being to invest in your own development. That caring, combined with the practical tools and frameworks ahead, will serve as your compass through the inevitable challenges and uncertainties of management.

The people you lead are counting on you—not to be perfect, but to be thoughtful, genuine, and committed to creating conditions where they can thrive. That's exactly what this book will help you do. Let's get started together.

I

Part I: Finding Your Leadership Foundation

Personal foundation and emotional transition
Master the internal work of becoming a manager—from navigating the emotional shift of your new role to building the self-awareness, confidence, and vision that will guide your leadership journey.

1

Welcome to Management: The Emotional Shift

Moving into management brings a new emotional world to navigate. It's common to go from excitement one day to doubt the next, all while figuring out how you fit in this new role and what kind of leader you want to be.

This chapter explores what happens emotionally when you step up as a manager for the first time. You'll learn about identity shifts, dealing with self-doubt, managing your feelings during tough moments, and finding tools that help you grow strong and steady as a leader.

The Psychology Behind the Transition

Research in organizational psychology shows that promotion to management triggers "role transition stress"—a period where your brain is literally rewiring itself to accommodate new responsibilities, relationships, and ways of thinking about work.

Dr. Sarah Chen, a workplace psychologist at Stanford, explains: "When someone becomes a manager, they're not just learning new tasks. They're fundamentally changing their professional identity, which affects everything from how they view their daily priorities to how they relate to former peers."

This neurological rewiring manifests in several predictable ways:

Cognitive Load Increase: Your brain is processing more complex information—not just your own tasks, but your team's performance, organizational dynamics, and strategic considerations. This mental workload can be exhausting until new neural pathways become established.

Social Identity Reorganization: Your relationships with colleagues shift dramatically. Former peers may treat you differently, and you may feel caught between your team and upper management. This social restructuring creates uncertainty about where you belong.

Decision-Making Pressure: The weight of decisions affecting other people's work lives, career development, and job satisfaction creates psychological pressure that individual contributors rarely experience.

Understanding these psychological foundations helps normalize the emotional turbulence of early management. You're not struggling because you're inadequate—you're adapting to one of the most complex professional transitions possible.

From Peer to Leader: Navigating Identity Transitions

The shift from colleague to manager involves fundamental changes in how you see yourself and how others see you. This transition often feels abrupt, even when you've been preparing for it.

The Impostor Syndrome Reality

Nearly every new manager experiences impostor syndrome—the feeling that you don't deserve your position or that you'll be "found out" as inadequate. This isn't a character flaw; it's a natural response to taking on responsibilities that feel larger than your current skill set.

Impostor syndrome in management often manifests as:

- **Questioning decisions** long after they've been made

- **Over-preparing** for meetings or conversations out of fear of appearing incompetent
- **Minimizing achievements** or attributing success to luck rather than capability
- **Avoiding difficult conversations** because you don't feel qualified to address them

The antidote to impostor syndrome isn't false confidence—it's realistic self-assessment combined with commitment to growth. You were promoted because someone saw leadership potential in you. Trust that judgment while acknowledging you have skills to develop.

The Authority Paradox

New managers often struggle with what researchers call the "authority paradox"—you have formal authority but may lack the experience or relationships that make that authority feel legitimate. Your title gives you the right to make decisions, but earning the respect that makes those decisions effective takes time.

This creates a delicate balance: You need to exercise authority to do your job effectively, but over-reliance on positional power can damage relationships and reduce your influence. The most effective approach involves:

Earning Authority Through Competence: Focus on making good decisions, supporting your team effectively, and delivering results. Authority earned through performance is more sustainable than authority imposed through title.

Transparent Learning: Acknowledge when you're learning something new and ask for input from experienced team members. This demonstrates humility while showing commitment to improvement.

Gradual Confidence Building: Start with smaller decisions and conversations to build your confidence and credibility before tackling the most challenging leadership situations.

Letting Go of Previous Identity

One of the most difficult aspects of the management transition involves releasing your identity as an individual contributor. If you excelled in your previous role, you may feel tempted to continue doing that work alongside your management responsibilities.

This transition requires conscious effort:

Accepting Different Success Metrics: Your success is now measured by your team's performance, not just your individual output. This shift can feel uncomfortable initially but represents the essence of leadership impact.

Redefining Value Contribution: Instead of creating work product directly, you create value by enabling others to be more effective, removing obstacles, and developing capabilities.

Managing the Skill Maintenance Balance: While you don't want to micromanage your former responsibilities, maintaining some technical competence helps you understand your team's challenges and maintain credibility.

Managing Emotional Reactions and Self-Doubt

Management triggers a wider range of emotions than most individual contributor roles. Learning to recognize, understand, and manage these emotional responses is crucial for sustained effectiveness.

Common Emotional Patterns

Decision Anxiety: The weight of making choices that affect other people can create persistent anxiety, especially when you lack complete information or when different stakeholders have competing interests.

Performance Pressure: Feeling responsible for your team's results while having less direct control over outcomes creates unique stress that individual contributors rarely experience.

Relationship Tension: Navigating changing dynamics with former peers, managing up to your boss, and building trust with new team members requires emotional energy and can create ongoing tension.

Isolation: Many new managers report feeling caught between their team and upper management, belonging fully to neither group.

Emotional Regulation Strategies

Mindful Awareness: Pay attention to your emotional responses without judgment. Notice what situations trigger anxiety, frustration, or self-doubt. This awareness is the first step in developing emotional intelligence.

Cognitive Reframing: When you notice negative thought patterns, examine them for accuracy. Instead of "I have no idea what I'm doing," try "I'm learning skills that take time to develop, and that's normal."

Support Network Development: Build relationships with other managers who understand your challenges. Peer mentoring and management support groups provide outlets for processing difficult experiences.

Stress Management Practices: Develop consistent practices for managing stress—whether through exercise, meditation, journaling, or other techniques that help you maintain emotional equilibrium.

Building Resilience Through Self-Compassion

Research by Dr. Kristin Neff shows that self-compassion—treating yourself with the same kindness you'd show a good friend facing challenges—actually increases resilience and performance more than self-criticism.

For new managers, self-compassion involves:
Acknowledging Universal Struggle: Recognize that every manager faces similar challenges during their transition. Your struggles don't indicate personal inadequacy but rather the universal difficulty of learning complex new skills.

Practicing Self-Kindness: Treat mistakes as learning opportunities rather than evidence of incompetence. The internal dialogue you maintain with yourself significantly affects your confidence and decision-making quality.

Maintaining Perspective: Remember that management skills develop over months and years, not weeks. Be patient with your progress while maintaining commitment to improvement.

Tools for Building Emotional Intelligence and Resilience

Emotional intelligence—the ability to recognize, understand, and manage emotions in yourself and others—is perhaps the most important capability for management success.

Self-Awareness Development

Daily Emotional Check-ins: Spend a few minutes each day reflecting on your emotional state and what triggered different feelings. This builds awareness of your emotional patterns.

Values Clarification: Identify your core values and notice when situations create internal conflict. Understanding your values helps you make decisions that feel authentic and sustainable.

Strengths and Growth Areas Assessment: Honestly evaluate your current capabilities while identifying specific areas for development. This balanced perspective reduces anxiety while maintaining focus on improvement.

Emotional Regulation Techniques

The Pause Practice: When facing intense emotions or difficult situations, practice taking a deliberate pause before responding. This brief moment allows for more thoughtful responses rather than reactive decisions.

Perspective Taking: When frustrated with team members or situations, practice seeing the situation from other perspectives. This reduces emotional reactivity and often reveals new solutions.

Energy Management: Pay attention to what activities and interactions energize you versus drain you. Structure your schedule to maximize energy for your most important leadership activities.

Building Team Emotional Intelligence

Modeling Emotional Awareness: Share appropriate insights about your own emotional responses to situations. This demonstrates that acknowledging emotions is professional and helpful.

Creating Psychological Safety: Establish team norms that make it safe for people to express concerns, admit mistakes, and ask questions without fear of judgment or retribution.

Emotional Contagion Awareness: Recognize that your emotional state affects your team's mood and performance. Consciously model the emotional tone you want to create.

The Timeline of Emotional Adjustment

Research suggests that emotional adjustment to management follows a predictable pattern:

Months 1-2: Honeymoon and Reality Shock Initial excitement gives way to the reality of daily management challenges. Emotional volatility is highest during this period.

Months 3-4: Competence Building You begin developing management-specific skills and confidence. Emotional swings become less dramatic and more manageable.

Months 5-6: Integration Your management identity begins to solidify. You find your leadership style and develop systems that work for you.

Months 7-12: Stabilization Emotional reactions become more predictable and manageable. You develop instincts for handling common situations.

Understanding this timeline provides reassurance during the most challenging early months. The emotional intensity you're experiencing is temporary and purposeful—your psyche is doing the work of integration and growth.

The emotional journey of becoming a manager is complex, personal, and entirely normal. By understanding the psychological foundations of this transition, developing tools for emotional awareness and regulation, and honoring both the challenges and opportunities of your new role, you're building the emotional intelligence that distinguishes effective leaders.

These emotional management skills aren't just personal development—they're the foundation for everything else you'll learn about leadership. You can't build trust with others if you haven't developed self-awareness. You can't navigate difficult conversations if you're hijacked by your own emotional reactions. You can't create psychological safety for others if you haven't learned to manage your own vulnerabilities.

This Week's Challenge

Start a simple emotional awareness practice: At the end of each workday, spend five minutes reflecting on:

- What emotions did I experience today?
- What triggered those emotions?
- How did my emotional state affect my interactions with others?
- What can I learn from these patterns?

Keep notes for one week and notice what patterns emerge.

* * *

Next Chapter Preview: In Chapter 2, we'll explore how to lay the foundations of ethical leadership, building on the emotional awareness you've developed to establish your core values, understand the distinction between leadership and management, and create a principled approach that'll guide all your future decisions as a leader.

2

Laying the Foundations of Leadership

Laying the foundations of leadership means facing new challenges, building fresh skills, and growing into a role that isn't always comfortable at first. For many, stepping up comes with doubts—about being accepted, making the right choices, or simply keeping up.

This chapter explores what sets leadership apart from management and why both matter for your growth. You'll find practical ways to build trust, act with empathy, and turn your values into daily habits. Ethical and thoughtful leadership isn't just possible—it's something you can start practicing today.

The Evolution of Leadership Thinking

Before diving into practical distinctions between leadership and management, it's worth understanding how our conception of effective leadership has evolved. The command-and-control models that dominated the industrial age—where managers were expected to have all the answers and employees simply followed orders—have proven inadequate for today's knowledge-based, rapidly changing work environments.

Modern leadership research has shifted toward "transformational leadership"—an approach that focuses on inspiring and developing others rather than simply directing their activities. This evolution reflects a fundamental change in what organizations need from their leaders: not just task completion, but innovation, adaptability, and employee engagement.

Dr. Amy Edmondson's research on psychological safety has further refined our understanding of effective leadership. Her studies show that teams perform best when leaders create environments where people feel safe to speak up, ask questions, and admit mistakes. This requires emotional intelligence, collaborative decision-making, and the ability to inspire others toward shared goals.

Understanding this context helps explain why many new managers feel uncertain about their role. You're learning to lead in an era that demands more sophisticated capabilities than traditional hierarchical management. This is both more challenging and more rewarding than previous generations experienced.

Leadership Versus Management: The Essentials

Understanding how leadership and management differ in practice helps anchor your sense of purpose as you step into greater responsibility.

The Nature of Leadership

Leadership centers on vision and inspiration. Consider a department facing rapid industry changes. A leader doesn't simply tell the team to work harder; instead, they paint a picture of future success and outline why each person's contributions matter. For example, a sales team struggling with new technology may feel overwhelmed. A leader inspires hope by showing the benefits this technology brings and connecting those advantages to each member's goals.

This visionary aspect goes beyond simply setting goals. It involves helping people understand the "why" behind their work—how their individual contributions connect to something larger and meaningful. Research by Simon Sinek demonstrates that people are most motivated when they understand not just what they're doing, but why it matters.

Consider the difference between these approaches:

- **Manager:** "We need to increase customer satisfaction scores by 15% this quarter."
- **Leader:** "Every interaction we have with customers is an opportunity to solve a real problem in someone's day. When we get it right, we're not just hitting numbers—we're making people's lives a little bit easier."

Both messages convey the same goal, but the leadership approach connects to purpose and meaning.

Inspiration separates leadership from authority. Rather than relying on job title, leaders build trust through actions and words. Consider a project launch where anxiety runs high. Instead of issuing demands, a strong leader acknowledges team concerns, listens actively, and highlights achievements, turning setbacks into learning moments. These encouraging behaviors foster genuine commitment rather than forced compliance.

The Strategic vs. Tactical Distinction

Leadership involves strategic thinking—the ability to see patterns, anticipate changes, and position the team for future success. While managers focus on executing today's priorities, leaders constantly scan the horizon for opportunities and threats. This doesn't mean leaders ignore current operations, but rather that they balance immediate needs with long-term vision.

Another hallmark of leadership lies in developing others. Leaders spot potential in their teams and create opportunities for growth. They might delegate challenging tasks to help someone stretch or regularly ask probing questions that push people to think deeply and solve problems creatively.

The Nature of Management

Management focuses on execution, systems, and results. When a project falls behind schedule, a manager analyzes the workflow, reallocates resources, and adjusts timelines to get back on track. This systematic approach ensures that day-to-day operations run smoothly and objectives are met.

Management excels at bringing order to complexity. Consider a product launch with multiple moving parts: marketing campaigns, inventory coordination, sales training, and customer support preparation. A skilled manager creates detailed project plans, assigns clear responsibilities, establishes check-in points, and monitors progress against deadlines.

Accountability drives management effectiveness. Managers track performance metrics, conduct regular reviews, and ensure team members understand expectations. They create structures that help people succeed and address issues before they become problems.

Quality management also involves resource optimization—ensuring teams have the tools, information, and support needed to perform well while eliminating waste and inefficiency.

The Integration Imperative

The strongest leaders seamlessly integrate both leadership and management capabilities, applying each approach when it's most needed. During a crisis, you might need to provide inspiring leadership while also implementing detailed management processes. When launching a new initiative, you'll need visionary leadership to gain buy-in and systematic management to ensure execution.

Neither approach is superior—they're complementary. The key is developing judgment to know which approach fits the moment.

First Principles for Ethical, Empathetic Leadership

These core principles of integrity, empathy, and respect form the ethical backbone of leadership. Each principle supports and strengthens the others, resulting in workplaces where people feel valued and teams achieve more collectively.

The Foundation of Integrity

Integrity encompasses consistency between values, words, and actions. When leaders demonstrate integrity, they create predictability and safety for their teams. People know what to expect, which reduces anxiety and increases trust.

Honesty builds credibility. Leaders who speak truthfully, admit mistakes, and share information openly become trustworthy in their teams' eyes. When a manager explains the reasons behind a tough decision, even if the news is disappointing, employees are more likely to respect both the choice and the leader.

Consistency in behavior means your team can predict how you'll respond to different situations. This doesn't mean being rigid, but rather being reliable in your core principles and decision-making approach.

Taking responsibility for both successes and failures demonstrates maturity and builds team confidence. When something goes wrong, effective leaders focus on solutions rather than blame.

Practicing Empathy in Leadership

Empathy—the ability to understand and share others' feelings—is crucial for building strong relationships and making informed decisions that consider human impact.

Active listening involves giving full attention to what team members say, asking clarifying questions, and reflecting back what you've heard. This demonstrates respect and often reveals insights that improve decision-making.

Perspective-taking means considering how decisions and changes affect different team members based on their roles, experience levels, and personal circumstances.

Emotional validation doesn't mean agreeing with every feeling, but rather acknowledging that people's emotional responses are real and important, even when you need to maintain certain decisions or standards.

Building Respect Through Actions

Respect in leadership goes beyond politeness—it involves recognizing the inherent worth and capabilities of every team member.

Recognizing contributions means acknowledging both large accomplishments and small efforts that move the team forward. Public recognition can be particularly powerful for building both individual confidence and team morale.

Investing in development demonstrates respect for people's potential and career aspirations. This might involve providing challenging assignments, supporting training opportunities, or offering mentoring.

Inclusive decision-making means seeking input from affected team members when appropriate and explaining decisions even when input can't be incorporated.

Developing Your Personal Leadership Philosophy

Your leadership philosophy serves as your North Star—guiding decisions when you face complex situations or competing priorities. This philosophy should reflect your values while being practical enough to apply in daily management situations.

Values-Based Decision Making

Identifying core values requires honest self-reflection. What principles do you never want to compromise? Common leadership values include integrity, fairness, growth, excellence, collaboration, and innovation. Your specific combination creates your unique leadership identity.

Testing values under pressure reveals their true strength. Consider past situations where you felt proud of your decisions versus times you felt regret. What values were honored or violated in each case?

Communicating values clearly helps your team understand what drives your decisions and what they can expect from your leadership. This doesn't require grand speeches—it's often more effective through consistent actions and brief explanations of your reasoning.

Creating Your Leadership Manifesto

A leadership manifesto is a personal document that articulates your beliefs about effective leadership, your commitments to your team, and the standards you hold for yourself.

Consider including statements about:

- **How you'll treat team members** during both good times and challenges
- **Your approach to decision-making** and how you'll involve others
- **Your commitment to development** (both your own and your team's)
- **How you'll handle mistakes** and what you expect from others
- **Your communication principles** and how you'll share information

This manifesto serves as both a personal reminder and a tool for sharing your leadership approach with your team.

Balancing Confidence and Humility

Effective leadership requires confidence to make decisions and take action, combined with humility to acknowledge limitations and continue learning.

Confident humility means being secure enough in your capabilities to admit when you don't know something and to seek help when needed. This actually increases rather than decreases your credibility with team members.

Learning orientation demonstrates that you view challenges as opportunities for growth rather than threats to your competence. This models the mindset you want your team to adopt.

Vulnerability with boundaries means sharing appropriate struggles and uncertainties while maintaining the confidence and stability your team needs to feel secure.

Practical Applications

Daily Leadership Practices

Morning intention setting: Begin each day by reflecting on what kind of leader you want to be today and what values you want to embody in your interactions.

Decision reflection: After making significant decisions, briefly consider whether your choice aligned with your values and what you might do differently in similar future situations.

Team member check-ins: Regular informal conversations with team members build relationships and provide opportunities to demonstrate empathy and support.

End-of-day review: Spend a few minutes reflecting on your leadership moments during the day—what went well and what you'd like to improve.

Building Your Leadership Presence

Consistent communication style: Develop a communication approach that feels authentic to you while being clear and respectful to others.

Physical presence: Pay attention to how your posture, facial expressions, and energy level affect team interactions. Small adjustments can significantly impact how others experience your leadership.

Emotional regulation: Practice managing your emotional responses, especially during stressful situations. Your team takes cues from your emotional state.

Follow-through reliability: Consistently doing what you say you'll do builds trust and demonstrates integrity in action.

This Week's Challenge

Draft your initial leadership philosophy by answering these questions:

- What are my top 5 core values?
- How do I want team members to describe my leadership style?
- What kind of team culture do I want to create?
- How will I handle mistakes (both my own and others')?
- What does success look like for me as a leader?

Share appropriate parts of your philosophy with your team and ask for their feedback.

* * *

Next Chapter Preview: In Chapter 3, we'll dive deep into building self-awareness and managerial confidence, providing specific tools for understanding your strengths, addressing development areas, and maintaining effectiveness under pressure.

3

Building Self-Awareness and Managerial Confidence

Building self-awareness as a manager is both an ongoing process and a real advantage in today's fast-paced workplaces. It often means taking a closer look at your own habits, reactions, and the patterns you may not even realize shape how you show up for your team.

This chapter provides practical tools to help you understand where you naturally lead with confidence—and where blind spots might be holding you back. You'll explore strategies for bouncing back from setbacks, managing stress, and using honest feedback to grow into a more resilient, trusted leader.

The Science of Self-Awareness in Leadership

Self-awareness isn't just a buzzword—it's a measurable competency that directly impacts leadership effectiveness. Research by organizational psychologist Tasha Eurich reveals that while 95% of people think they're self-aware, only 10-15% actually are. This gap becomes particularly problematic for new managers, who must understand their own triggers, biases, and motivations before they can effectively guide others.

Dr. Daniel Goleman's work on emotional intelligence identifies self-awareness as the foundation of all other emotional competencies. Without it, you can't regulate your emotions, empathize with others, or manage relationships effectively. For managers, this translates into practical challenges: How can you give constructive feedback if you don't recognize your own defensive reactions? How can you build trust if you're unaware of behaviors that undermine credibility?

Brain imaging studies show that people with higher self-awareness have more active prefrontal cortexes—the brain region responsible for executive function, decision-making, and emotional regulation. This suggests that developing self-awareness literally changes your brain's capacity for effective leadership.

Understanding this scientific foundation helps explain why self-awareness work feels challenging. You're not just changing habits—you're rewiring neural pathways that have been reinforced for years. The good news is that neuroplasticity means these changes are possible at any age, with consistent practice and intentional effort.

Recognizing Your Strengths and Blind Spots

Understanding your own leadership tendencies is crucial for every new manager. When you become aware of the strengths you naturally bring, as well as the biases and blind spots that can disrupt team cohesion, you lay the foundation for genuine trust and psychological safety. The way you show up in conversations—how you listen, give feedback, or make decisions—signals to your team whether their voices matter.

The Power of Personality Frameworks

Personality frameworks like DiSC or MBTI help clarify your communication style and how you approach problems and relationships. These assessments aren't about putting people in boxes; rather, they illuminate patterns that affect your leadership effectiveness.

For example, someone with a DiSC Dominance style may excel at setting bold goals and driving for results, but sometimes pushes forward without pausing to hear quieter voices. A person with the Steadiness style will likely prioritize harmony and patience, but might avoid making tough calls that could upset the group.

The Five Voices framework offers another useful lens, identifying distinct communication styles: Pioneer (big-picture visionary), Connector (relational bridge-builder), Creative (innovative challenger), Guardian (operational executor), and Nurturer (supportive advocate). Understanding your primary voice helps explain why certain leadership situations feel natural while others drain your energy.

Consider a manager who loves brainstorming grand visions but overlooks important details—this could signal a Pioneer or Creative voice. Alternatively, a Guardian-style manager might be thorough and reliable but risk slowing progress by over-analyzing or hesitating to take bold steps.

Identifying Your Leadership Triggers

Beyond personality patterns, understanding your emotional triggers is crucial for maintaining effectiveness under pressure. Common leadership triggers include:

Criticism or Questioning: Some managers become defensive when their decisions are challenged, leading to shut-down conversations rather than productive dialogue.

Uncertainty and Ambiguity: Managers who prefer clear parameters may struggle with the inherent ambiguity of leadership roles, leading to over-control or decision paralysis.

Conflict and Tension: Some leaders avoid necessary difficult conversations due to discomfort with interpersonal conflict.

Perfectionism: Managers who hold themselves to impossibly high standards may micromanage their teams or delay decisions waiting for perfect information.

Recognition and Validation: Leaders who need frequent acknowledgment may make decisions based on popularity rather than effectiveness.

Recognizing your triggers allows you to pause and choose your response rather than reacting automatically. This awareness is the first step in developing emotional regulation skills essential for leadership effectiveness.

Seeking and Processing Feedback

One of the most powerful tools for building self-awareness is systematic feedback collection. However, many new managers either avoid feedback due to anxiety or collect it ineffectively.

360-Degree Feedback Process: Create structured opportunities to gather input from your boss, peers, and team members. Use specific questions like:

- "What should I start doing to be more effective?"
- "What should I stop doing that isn't serving the team well?"
- "What should I continue doing that's working?"

Regular Check-ins: Build feedback into your routine interactions rather than waiting for formal reviews. Simple questions like "How am I doing as your manager?" or "What could I do differently to support you better?" open important conversations.

Feedback Processing Strategy: When receiving feedback, practice these responses:

- **Listen without defending:** Your first job is to understand, not to justify
- **Ask clarifying questions:** Seek specific examples to understand the feedback fully
- **Thank the person:** Acknowledge their courage in sharing honest input
- **Reflect before responding:** Take time to process feedback before deciding how to act on it

Aisha's Retail Reality Check

Aisha became a store manager at 26, promoted from sales associate after consistently exceeding targets. However, within six months, employee turnover spiked to 40%—well above industry averages.

The Wake-Up Call: During her quarterly review, Aisha's district manager shared concerning feedback from exit interviews. Former employees described her as "demanding," "never satisfied," and "impossible to please." Aisha was shocked—she thought her high standards would inspire excellence.

Self-Awareness Journey: Rather than dismissing the feedback, Aisha requested 360-degree feedback from current team members. The results revealed that her direct communication style, which customers appreciated, felt harsh and critical to staff. Her focus on metrics came across as caring more about numbers than people.

Blind Spot Discovery: Aisha realized she had been managing others the way she liked to be managed—with direct feedback and high expectations. She hadn't considered that different people needed different approaches to feel supported and motivated.

Growth in Action: Aisha adapted her leadership style while maintaining her standards:

- **Recognition First:** She began every feedback conversation by acknowledging what the person was doing well
- **Collaborative Goal-Setting:** Instead of simply announcing targets, she asked team members for input on realistic goals
- **Individual Adaptation:** She learned each team member's communication preferences and adjusted her approach accordingly
- **Personal Investment:** She started having brief personal check-ins with each employee, learning about their goals and challenges

Results: Within four months, turnover dropped to 15%—below industry average. Customer satisfaction scores improved as happier employees provided better service. Sales increased 12% as the team became more engaged and collaborative.

Key Learning: Aisha discovered that self-awareness isn't just about understanding yourself—it's about understanding how your natural style affects others and adapting accordingly without losing your authentic leadership voice.

Building Emotional Resilience

Leadership involves constant emotional challenges—difficult conversations, disappointing results, team conflicts, and organizational pressures. Building emotional resilience helps you maintain effectiveness even during tough periods.

Understanding Emotional Resilience

Emotional resilience isn't about being unaffected by challenges—it's about recovering quickly from setbacks and maintaining perspective during difficult times. Resilient leaders experience the full range of emotions but don't let those emotions derail their decision-making or team leadership.

Components of Emotional Resilience:
Emotional Awareness: Recognizing your emotional state in real-time and understanding what triggered those emotions.
Emotional Regulation: The ability to manage intense emotions without being overwhelmed or reactive.
Perspective Maintenance: Keeping challenges in context and maintaining focus on long-term goals despite short-term setbacks.
Recovery Speed: Bouncing back quickly from disappointments or failures without getting stuck in rumination or self-blame.
Stress Tolerance: Maintaining effectiveness under pressure without burnout or decision fatigue.

Practical Resilience-Building Strategies

Mindfulness and Present-Moment Awareness: Develop the habit of checking in with yourself throughout the day. Simple questions like "What am I feeling right now?" and "What does my body need?" build emotional awareness and prevent stress accumulation.

Cognitive Reframing: Practice viewing challenges as opportunities for growth rather than threats to your competence. Instead of "This is a disaster," try "This is a complex situation that will help me develop new skills."

Stress Inoculation: Gradually expose yourself to increasingly challenging situations in low-stakes environments. This builds confidence and coping skills for when high-pressure situations arise.

Recovery Rituals: Develop consistent practices that help you recover from difficult days—whether that's exercise, meditation, time in nature, or conversations with trusted friends.

Support Network Development: Build relationships with other managers who understand your challenges. Peer support groups, mentoring relationships, and professional coaching provide outlets for processing difficult experiences.

Managing Impostor Syndrome

Nearly every new manager experiences impostor syndrome—the feeling that you don't deserve your position or that you'll be "found out" as inadequate. This isn't a character flaw; it's a natural response to taking on responsibilities that feel larger than your current skill set.

Reframing Impostor Syndrome: Instead of viewing self-doubt as evidence of incompetence, recognize it as evidence that you care about doing well and are aware of areas for growth. The most dangerous managers are those who are overconfident and unaware of their limitations.

Evidence-Based Self-Assessment: Keep a record of your accomplishments, positive feedback, and successful decisions. During moments of self-doubt, review this evidence to maintain a balanced perspective on your capabilities.

Growth Mindset Application: Adopt Carol Dweck's growth mindset by viewing your current limitations as temporary rather than permanent. Instead of "I don't know how to handle this," try "I don't know how to handle this yet."

Developing a Learning Agility Mindset

In today's rapidly changing business environment, the ability to learn quickly and adapt to new situations is more valuable than existing knowledge or experience. Learning agility involves four key dimensions:

Mental Agility: Thinking critically and examining problems from multiple angles. This means questioning assumptions, looking for patterns, and considering various solutions before acting.

People Agility: Understanding and working effectively with diverse personalities and situations. This includes reading social dynamics, adapting communication styles, and building relationships across differences.

Change Agility: Embracing ambiguity and being willing to experiment with new approaches. This involves comfort with uncertainty and resilience when experiments don't work as expected.

Results Agility: Delivering results in challenging circumstances by building teams and inspiring others. This combines all other forms of agility to achieve outcomes even when conditions are difficult.

Creating a Personal Learning Plan

Monthly Learning Goals: Identify one specific skill or knowledge area to focus on each month. This might be conflict resolution, strategic thinking, or industry knowledge.

Learning Methods: Diversify how you acquire new knowledge:

- Books and articles for theoretical foundations
- Podcasts and videos for convenience and variety
- Conferences and workshops for immersive learning
- Mentorship and coaching for personalized guidance
- Stretch assignments for experiential learning

Application Opportunities: Deliberately practice new skills in low-risk situations before applying them to high-stakes scenarios.

Reflection and Integration: Regularly assess what you've learned and how it's changing your leadership effectiveness.

Robert's Remote Revelation

Robert, a 45-year-old operations manager with 15 years of traditional office management experience, suddenly found himself leading a distributed team across three time zones when his company shifted to remote work.

The Challenge: Robert's leadership style relied heavily on visual cues— reading body language, having impromptu conversations, and managing through physical presence. He felt lost without these familiar tools and noticed team engagement dropping.

Self-Awareness Moment: During a particularly ineffective video call where team members seemed disengaged, Robert realized his traditional approach wasn't working. Instead of blaming remote work or his team, he asked himself what he needed to learn.

Learning Agility in Action:

- **Mental Agility:** Robert studied remote leadership best practices and questioned his assumptions about what effective management required
- **People Agility:** He reached out to successful remote managers in other departments to understand their approaches
- **Change Agility:** He experimented with new communication tools and meeting formats, accepting that some attempts would fail
- **Results Agility:** He focused on outcomes rather than activity, developing new metrics for team effectiveness

Adaptation Strategies:

- **Asynchronous Communication:** Robert learned to communicate clearly in writing and use project management tools effectively
- **Intentional Relationship Building:** He scheduled regular one-on-one video calls to maintain personal connections
- **Digital Body Language:** He developed skills in reading engagement through video calls and written communication
- **Flexible Scheduling:** He adapted his availability to accommodate team members across time zones

Results: Within three months, Robert's team scored highest in the company for remote work satisfaction. Productivity increased 18% as he learned to leverage the advantages of distributed work rather than fighting against them.

Key Learning: Robert discovered that learning agility—the willingness to adapt and acquire new skills—was more valuable than his years of traditional management experience when circumstances changed dramatically.

Understanding the science of self-awareness, developing emotional resilience, and cultivating a growth mindset creates a powerful foundation for effective leadership. These internal capabilities support every external skill you'll develop—from communication and trust-building to strategic thinking and team development.

The self-awareness work you're doing now isn't just personal development; it's an investment in your team's success. Leaders who understand themselves can better understand others, creating the psychological safety and trust that high-performing teams require.

This Week's Challenge

Complete a comprehensive self-awareness assessment:

1. **Take a personality assessment** (DiSC, MBTI, or Five Voices) and reflect on how your natural style affects your team interactions
2. **Request feedback** from three people: your boss, a peer, and a team member, using the specific questions provided in this chapter
3. **Identify your top 2 emotional triggers** and develop a plan for managing them more effectively
4. **Create a personal learning goal** for the next month with specific actions and success metrics

* * *

Next Chapter Preview: In Chapter 4, we'll explore how to create and communicate vision that inspires your team and provides clear direction for collective effort.

4

Creating and Communicating Vision

Creating and sharing vision with a team is something every leader faces, no matter how much experience they have. It's natural to wonder if you're getting it right or worry that your message might not land the way you hope.

This chapter walks you through building a vision that actually means something to your team and making sure everyone understands where you're headed together. You'll get practical ideas for involving your people in shaping direction, communicating with impact, and checking that your key messages are truly heard.

The Psychology of Vision and Meaning

Humans are meaning-making creatures—we need to understand not just what we're doing, but why it matters. This need becomes even more pronounced in work environments where people spend significant portions of their lives.

Research by Viktor Frankl demonstrated that people can endure almost anything if they have a sense of purpose. His work laid the foundation for what organizational psychologists now call "meaning-making at work"—the process through which employees connect their daily tasks to broader significance.

Dr. Adam Grant's studies at Wharton further illuminate this connection.

In one famous experiment, he arranged for scholarship recipients to briefly speak with university fundraising callers about how the scholarships had changed their lives. This simple intervention increased fundraising performance by 400% because callers could directly see the impact of their work.

The Three Levels of Meaning at Work:
Personal Meaning: How the work connects to individual values, interests, and career aspirations.
Relational Meaning: How the work affects colleagues, customers, and communities—the human impact of daily efforts.
Purpose Meaning: How the work contributes to something larger than immediate tasks or even individual careers.

Effective vision creation addresses all three levels, helping team members see how their individual contributions serve personal growth, strengthen relationships, and advance meaningful purposes.

The Neuroscience of Motivation

When people understand the "why" behind their work, their brains release dopamine—the neurotransmitter associated with motivation and reward. This isn't just about feeling good; it's about sustained engagement and performance over time.

Vision also activates what neuroscientists call the "seeking system"—the brain's drive to explore, learn, and pursue goals. When people can visualize a compelling future state and understand their role in achieving it, this system energizes them toward action.

This scientific understanding explains why generic mission statements often fail to motivate. Abstract language like "excellence" or "customer focus" doesn't create vivid mental images or emotional connections. Effective vision paints specific pictures of success that people can see, feel, and work toward.

Elements of Compelling Vision

A compelling vision combines aspiration with clarity, painting a picture of success that feels both inspiring and achievable. The most effective visions share several characteristics:

Specificity and Clarity

Vague aspirations like "be the best" or "exceed expectations" don't provide actionable direction. Strong visions include specific details about what success looks like, how it will be measured, and what will be different when the vision is achieved.

Instead of: "We want to provide excellent customer service."
Try: "Every customer will complete their interaction feeling heard, helped, and valued, with 95% rating their experience as positive and recommending us to others."

Instead of: "We aim to be innovative."
Try: "We'll launch three new product features each quarter based on customer feedback, with each feature adopted by at least 60% of users within six months."

Emotional Resonance

People are motivated more by emotion than logic. Effective visions connect to feelings—pride in accomplishment, excitement about possibilities, satisfaction in helping others, or determination to overcome challenges.

Consider how different these approaches feel:
Logic-based: "Increasing efficiency by 20% will improve our quarterly margins."
Emotion-based: "When we eliminate the frustrations that slow us down,

we'll spend more time on the creative work that drew us to this field in the first place."

Personal Connection

Strong visions help individuals see how their unique skills and interests contribute to collective success. This requires understanding what motivates different team members and explicitly connecting vision elements to their aspirations.

For a diverse team, this might mean highlighting different aspects:

- **Growth-oriented team members:** Emphasizing learning opportunities and skill development
- **Relationship-focused individuals:** Highlighting collaboration and community impact
- **Achievement-driven people:** Focusing on measurable outcomes and recognition
- **Security-minded team members:** Emphasizing stability and sustainable success

Future-Focused Orientation

Vision describes a future state that doesn't yet exist but feels attainable with sustained effort. It should stretch the team beyond current capabilities while remaining grounded in realistic assessment of resources and constraints.

The time horizon matters too. Short-term visions (3-6 months) create urgency and quick wins. Medium-term visions (1-2 years) allow for significant development and change. Long-term visions (3-5 years) inspire transformational thinking and sustained commitment.

Collaborative Vision Development

The most powerful visions emerge from collaborative processes that engage team members in both creation and refinement. This isn't about consensus on every detail, but about ensuring the vision reflects collective wisdom and generates broad commitment.

Stakeholder Input Strategies

Vision Workshops: Structured brainstorming sessions where team members answer prompts like "What impact do we want to have in our industry?" or "How should success look for our clients and community?"
Anonymous Surveys: Collect honest input without fear of judgment, then share themes and guide the group toward consensus.
Cross-Functional Collaboration: Include voices from different backgrounds to ensure diverse perspectives contribute unique insights.

Vision Workshop Structure:

1. **Individual Reflection** (15 minutes): Team members privately consider what excites them about the team's potential
2. **Small Group Sharing** (30 minutes): Groups of 3-4 people share reflections and identify common themes
3. **Theme Synthesis** (20 minutes): Groups report themes to the larger group; facilitator captures patterns
4. **Collaborative Drafting** (45 minutes): Entire team works together to craft vision statement incorporating key themes
5. **Refinement** (ongoing): Take draft away for polishing, then bring back for final input

Managing Different Perspectives

Not everyone will initially share the same vision of success. Some team members may be more conservative while others push for radical change. Some focus on internal operations while others emphasize external impact.

Perspective Integration Techniques:
Find Common Ground: Identify shared values and goals that everyone can support, then build from that foundation.
Address Concerns Directly: When someone expresses skepticism, explore the underlying concerns rather than dismissing them.
Create Space for Dissent: Encourage honest discussion of different viewpoints to strengthen the final vision.
Pilot Testing: For significant vision elements, consider small-scale experiments to test assumptions before full commitment.

Jennifer's School District Transformation

Jennifer, a 38-year-old elementary school principal, faced the challenge of implementing new project-based learning methodologies while managing resistance from teachers comfortable with traditional approaches.

The Stakeholder Challenge: Her vision needed to align teachers (concerned about workload and student outcomes), parents (worried about academic standards), and administrators (focused on district-wide consistency and test scores).

Collaborative Vision Process:
Teacher Input Sessions: Jennifer held after-school workshops where teachers shared their educational philosophies and concerns about current teaching challenges. Rather than presenting project-based learning as the solution, she asked what changes would help them better serve students.
Parent Community Forums: She organized evening sessions where parents discussed their hopes for their children's education and shared concerns

about proposed changes. These conversations revealed that parents wanted engaged, curious learners more than high test scores.

Student Voice Integration: Jennifer conducted focus groups with students about what kinds of learning excited them most and when they felt most successful.

Administrative Alignment: She worked with district leadership to understand how building-level innovation could support system-wide goals.

Vision Development Outcome: The collaborative process revealed shared commitment to developing "confident, curious, collaborative learners who can solve real-world problems." This vision resonated because:

- **Teachers** saw it as honoring their expertise while providing growth opportunities
- **Parents** recognized it as preparing children for future success beyond test scores
- **Students** connected it to engaging, hands-on learning experiences
- **Administrators** understood it as innovative while maintaining academic rigor

Implementation Strategy: Jennifer used the collaboratively developed vision to guide decisions about curriculum, professional development, and resource allocation. When resistance arose, she referenced the shared vision rather than mandating compliance.

Results:

- 85% teacher adoption of project-based methods within one year
- Student engagement scores increased 30%
- Parent satisfaction with communication and involvement improved significantly
- The school became a district model for innovative teaching practices

Key Learning: Jennifer discovered that vision development is as important as the vision itself. When people participate in creating direction, they're much more likely to commit to achieving it.

Communication Strategies for Vision

Creating compelling vision is only half the challenge—communicating it effectively ensures everyone understands and commits to the shared direction.

Multi-Channel Communication Approach

People process information differently, so effective vision communication uses multiple channels and formats to ensure broad understanding.

Written Communication:

- Vision statements posted in common areas
- Email updates connecting daily work to vision progress
- Project documents that reference vision alignment
- Performance reviews that assess vision contribution

Verbal Communication:

- Team meetings that begin with vision reminders
- One-on-one conversations about individual vision connection
- Presentation opportunities that highlight vision progress
- Storytelling that makes vision tangible and relatable

Visual Communication:

- Infographics that illustrate vision components
- Dashboard displays showing progress toward vision metrics
- Photo displays of vision in action
- Video messages that convey emotional energy

Message Adaptation for Different Audiences

Effective communication goes beyond repetition—it involves tailoring content and style to the audience. Different team members need different levels of detail and different types of connection to the vision.

Audience Analysis Framework:
Technical Expertise Level:

- **High expertise:** Can handle detailed explanations and appreciate precision
- **Medium expertise:** Needs some context but can follow complex ideas
- **Low expertise:** Requires background information and simple language

Communication Style Preference:

- **Direct communicators:** Want bottom line first, then supporting details
- **Contextual communicators:** Need background and rationale before conclusions
- **Visual communicators:** Process information better with charts, diagrams, examples
- **Narrative communicators:** Connect with stories and analogies

Role-Based Priorities:

- **Execution-focused roles:** Need clear action steps and deadlines
- **Strategy-focused roles:** Want to understand broader implications and connections
- **People-focused roles:** Interested in impact on team members and relationships
- **Process-focused roles:** Concerned with workflow and systematic implementation

The Art of Contextual Communication

Providing context boosts clarity and buy-in. Sharing why certain directions were chosen—and which alternatives were considered but rejected—helps employees grasp the reasoning behind decisions.

Context-Rich Communication Structure:

1. **Situation:** What circumstances led to this decision/direction?
2. **Options:** What alternatives were considered?
3. **Criteria:** What factors influenced the choice?
4. **Decision:** What was chosen and why?
5. **Implementation:** How will this move forward?
6. **Success Metrics:** How will we measure progress?

Digital Communication Best Practices

Modern teams often work across locations and time zones, requiring thoughtful digital communication strategies.

Written Messages:

- Lead with key points for scannable communication
- Use formatting (bullets, bold, whitespace) to improve readability
- Include context links for detailed background information
- End with clear action items and deadlines

Video Messages:

- Keep recordings under 5 minutes for routine updates
- Use visual aids to support key points
- Include transcript or summary for accessibility
- Allow for questions through follow-up channels

Virtual Meetings:

- Start with vision reminder to frame discussion
- Use breakout rooms for small group processing
- Record key decisions and share afterwards
- Follow up with written summary of action items

Marcus's Tech Startup Pivot

Marcus, a 31-year-old CTO at a growing tech startup, faced the challenge of communicating a major product direction change to both technical and non-technical stakeholders.

The Communication Challenge: The company needed to pivot from their original consumer-focused app to a B2B platform—a change that affected everyone from engineers to sales teams to investors.

Multi-Stakeholder Approach:

Engineering Team: Marcus used technical architecture diagrams and code samples to show how existing work would transfer to the new direction. He emphasized the technical challenges and learning opportunities the pivot would create.

Sales Team: He focused on market opportunity data and customer feedback that drove the pivot decision. He provided specific talking points for customer conversations and competitive positioning.

Marketing Team: Marcus worked with them to develop new messaging frameworks and visual identity elements that would support the B2B positioning.

Leadership Team: He presented comprehensive business case analysis including financial projections, risk assessments, and implementation timelines.

Investor Communication: Marcus and the CEO jointly presented market research, competitive analysis, and revised growth projections that justified the strategic shift.

Communication Strategy:

- **Consistency:** Core message remained the same across audiences while details varied
- **Transparency:** Honest discussion of risks and challenges alongside opportunities
- **Involvement:** Each stakeholder group contributed input to implementation planning
- **Regular Updates:** Weekly progress reports during the transition period

Results:

- 95% team retention during a period when pivots often cause departures
- Successful product launch within six months of pivot decision
- Strong investor support including additional funding round
- Clear team alignment around new direction and priorities

Key Learning: Marcus learned that complex changes require both consistent core messaging and audience-specific adaptation. Success came from treating communication as an ongoing conversation rather than a one-time announcement.

Measuring Vision Effectiveness

Compelling vision must translate into measurable progress and observable behavior changes. Without metrics and feedback mechanisms, even the most inspiring vision can lose momentum over time.

Vision Metrics Framework

Awareness Metrics: Do people understand the vision?

- Vision recall surveys

- Team meeting discussions about vision connection
- Frequency of vision references in daily work

Engagement Metrics: Do people care about the vision?

- Employee engagement scores related to purpose and meaning
- Voluntary participation in vision-related initiatives
- Quality of contributions during vision discussions

Behavior Metrics: Are people acting in alignment with the vision?

- Decision-making patterns that reflect vision priorities
- Resource allocation choices that support vision goals
- Daily work activities that advance vision progress

Results Metrics: Is the vision producing desired outcomes?

- Specific performance indicators identified in the vision
- Customer or stakeholder feedback related to vision elements
- Long-term trend data showing movement toward vision state

Communication Effectiveness Assessment

Regular assessment of communication effectiveness ensures your vision messages are landing as intended.

Clarity Assessment:

- Can team members accurately summarize the vision in their own words?
- Do people understand how their work connects to vision achievement?
- Are there consistent interpretations across different team members?

Engagement Assessment:

- Do people speak positively about the vision during informal conversations?
- Are team members proactively identifying ways to advance the vision?
- Is there evidence of vision-driven initiative and innovation?

Application Assessment:

- Are people making decisions that align with vision priorities?
- Do project proposals and resource requests reference vision connection?
- Are there observable behavior changes that support vision progress?

The communication skills you're developing here form the foundation for building trust—our next crucial leadership competency. When people feel heard, understood, and clear about direction, they're much more likely to extend trust to their leader and commit fully to shared goals.

This Week's Challenge

Develop and communicate a vision for your team:

1. **Conduct stakeholder input** using one of the methods from this chapter
2. **Draft a vision statement** that incorporates collaborative feedback
3. **Create a communication plan** using multiple channels and audience-specific messaging
4. **Implement feedback mechanisms** to assess vision understanding and engagement
5. **Schedule regular check-ins** to maintain vision focus and adjust as needed

* * *

Next Chapter Preview: In Chapter 5, we'll explore how to build trust and credibility—the essential foundation that makes vision communication effective and enables all other leadership capabilities.

II

Part II: Building Essential Management Skills

Core interpersonal management skills

Develop the fundamental people skills every effective manager needs: earning trust, communicating with impact, developing talent, and creating inclusive team environments where everyone can thrive.

5

Building Trust and Credibility

Building trust as a new manager means finding ways to make your words match your actions while showing people you truly care about their success.

This chapter covers how to earn confidence step by step, recover when things go wrong, and use practical tools to strengthen relationships with your team.

The Science of Trust in Leadership

Trust is the fundamental currency that makes everything else possible. Without it, vision falls flat, communication feels hollow, and good intentions get lost in skepticism. Understanding how trust develops gives new managers a significant advantage in building strong, productive relationships.

Neuroscientist Paul Zak's research reveals that trust triggers the release of oxytocin, often called the "bonding hormone." When people trust their leader, their brains literally change—stress hormones decrease, cognitive performance improves, and collaborative instincts strengthen. This isn't just feel-good psychology; it's measurable brain chemistry that directly impacts team effectiveness.

Dr. Frances Frei from Harvard Business School identifies trust as having three core drivers: authenticity (people believe you're genuine), logic (people believe you have good judgment), and empathy (people believe you care about them). When any of these three wobbles, trust erodes. For new managers, this framework provides a clear roadmap for building credibility systematically.

The Trust Equation in Practice

Charles Green's trust equation offers another practical lens: Trust = (Credibility + Reliability + Intimacy) / Self-Orientation. In simple terms, trust grows when people see you as competent (credibility), consistent (reliability), and safe to be around (intimacy), while diminishing when they perceive you as primarily serving your own interests (high self-orientation).

For new managers, this equation explains why some relationships click immediately while others struggle. You might have strong technical credibility from your previous role, but if you're inconsistent in follow-through or seem more focused on looking good than supporting your team, trust will remain fragile.

Understanding these scientific foundations helps normalize the trust-building process. It's not about charisma or natural talent—it's about consistently demonstrating competence, reliability, and genuine care for others' success.

The Trust Equation: How New Managers Earn Credibility

Starting strong as a new manager means making your presence felt in ways that foster psychological safety for your team. The foundation you built through self-awareness (Chapter 3) and clear vision communication (Chapter 4) now becomes visible through consistent actions that demonstrate reliability and care.

Show Up, Consistently: The Power of Small Actions

Showing up consistently signals reliability and tells employees they can count on you. When you arrive on time for meetings, you send the message that everyone's time is valued. If your calendar says you're hosting open office hours each week, being at your desk and ready to engage during those times lets people know you're approachable. Reliable leaders also follow through on planned check-ins. For example, if you set a monthly one-on-one, do not cancel or reschedule unless absolutely necessary.

The power of consistency extends beyond punctuality to emotional presence. Teams notice when their manager is distracted, stressed, or disengaged. While you don't need to be artificially cheerful, maintaining a steady, professional demeanor helps create stability for others. This doesn't mean suppressing emotions—rather, it means managing them consciously so your mood doesn't become the team's weather.

Elena's Daily Routine: When Elena became project manager for a construction crew, she implemented a predictable daily routine: 6:30 AM safety briefing, hourly check-ins during critical operations, and end-of-day team updates. She made herself available exactly when she said she would and always followed through on commitments. When she promised to resolve a tools shortage by Tuesday, she had new equipment delivered Monday evening. This consistency helped her team know what to expect, creating psychological safety even in a high-pressure environment.

Responding to emails and messages within a defined period—say, within 24 hours for non-urgent items—helps maintain an atmosphere of responsiveness and support. This doesn't mean being available 24/7, but rather setting clear expectations about when people can expect to hear back from you. Some managers use auto-replies that say, "I'll respond to non-urgent emails within one business day" or "For urgent matters, please call or text."

These straightforward behaviors lay the groundwork for trust because your actions match your words and expectations feel stable. When people know what to expect from their manager, they can focus on their work rather than wondering about your availability or commitment.

Deliver on Promises: The Foundation of Reliability

Trust also grows every time a manager fulfills promises and handles mistakes deftly. Take a situation where you commit to providing feedback on a project by Friday. Meeting that deadline shows you respect your team's work and hold yourself to commitments.

When mistakes happen—and they will—the key is how you handle them. When honesty is your first response, employees can trust that they're getting the real story. Being open about where you went wrong develops credibility because people see that you have the character to admit errors and the competence to learn from them.

Kevin's Promise Recovery: Customer service manager Kevin learned this lesson when inheriting a demoralized team. His first week revealed employees had lost faith in management promises. Kevin started small—when he promised to move the printer closer to workstations, he did it within two days. When he said he'd institute "Solution of the Week" recognition, the first award went out the following Monday. These quick wins on small promises built credibility for larger commitments like advocating with corporate for policy changes.

The follow-through extends to acknowledging when promises can't be kept and providing alternative solutions. If you committed to getting budget approval for new software but the request was denied, explain what happened and offer alternatives. This transparency maintains trust even when outcomes aren't what the team hoped for.

Transparency in Intentions: Building Understanding Through Openness

Transparency doesn't mean sharing everything—some information must remain confidential—but it does mean sharing the reasoning behind decisions when possible. Instead of saying, "We're changing our project management system," try, "We're changing our project management system because our current one doesn't integrate with our client portal, which has been causing delays and duplicated work."

Make it a habit to discuss team goals openly so everyone sees how their efforts contribute to a common purpose. During difficult periods—like navigating an unexpected shift in customer needs or operational setbacks— communicate candidly about obstacles and invite input for solutions. Such transparency, supported by regular updates and honest conversations, conveys respect and establishes shared ownership over results.

The Transparency Framework:

- **What** is happening or changing
- **Why** it's necessary or beneficial
- **How** it will affect the team
- **When** changes will occur
- **Who** is responsible for what
- **Where** people can get more information or ask questions

This framework ensures comprehensive communication while maintaining appropriate boundaries.

Maya's Transparent Learning: When 26-year-old software engineer Maya was promoted to lead a team that included more experienced developers, she made her learning visible rather than trying to hide her inexperience. In team meetings, she would say things like: "I haven't managed a release this complex before. Tom, based on your experience, what should I be watching for?" This approach positioned her as someone confident enough to learn publicly while respecting the expertise around her.

Building Credibility Through Competence

While authenticity and reliability form the foundation of trust, competence—your ability to deliver results and make good decisions—provides the confidence people need to follow your lead. New managers often worry about appearing incompetent when they don't know something, but research shows that admitting knowledge gaps while demonstrating commitment to learning actually builds credibility.

Competence-Building Strategies:

Lead with Your Strengths: Identify areas where you have genuine expertise and make sure those strengths are visible to your team. If you excel at problem-solving, take the lead on complex challenges. If you're great at client relationships, be present during important customer interactions.

Elena knew her technical expertise was her strongest asset when facing skeptical construction workers. When the security vulnerability crisis hit Maya's team, she dove into the code review personally while coordinating the broader response: "I'm going to work on the authentication module fix while Tom handles the database queries and Sarah works on front-end validation."

Admit What You Don't Know: When faced with questions beyond your expertise, say "I don't know, but I'll find out" or "That's not my area of strength—who on the team has experience with this?" This honesty builds trust while positioning you as someone who prioritizes good outcomes over appearing smart.

When a worker questioned Elena about a structural modification, instead of simply citing engineering principles, she grabbed her hard hat and safety gear to physically examine the issue together. "Look, I know these blueprints like the back of my hand," she told the crew, "but you see things I miss from behind a desk. If something doesn't look right to you, I want to know immediately."

Learn Publicly: Share what you're learning about management, industry trends, or team needs. This might mean discussing insights from a management book you're reading or explaining new approaches you want to try. Public learning demonstrates growth mindset and vulnerability.

Make Good Decisions with Available Information: Competence isn't about having perfect information—it's about making sound judgments with what you have. Explain your decision-making process so people understand your reasoning even when outcomes aren't perfect.

When questions arose about load-bearing calculations that Elena couldn't answer immediately, she said, "I need to run the numbers properly before we proceed. Give me two hours, and I'll have a definitive answer with the calculations to show you." She always returned with detailed explanations and written documentation.

Emotional Intelligence in Trust Building

Trust building requires the emotional intelligence foundation from Chapter 3—reading situations, managing emotions, and responding appropriately to others' needs.

Reading the Room: Effective trust-building requires the active listening skills from Chapter 6: noticing team dynamics, acknowledging feelings before facts, and asking "What would be most helpful?"

Kevin applied this skill when he noticed his customer service representatives arriving exactly on time and leaving precisely at closing, with no voluntary collaboration. Instead of addressing this as a performance issue, he recognized it as a trust problem and scheduled individual conversations to understand the underlying dynamics.

Emotional Regulation: Your emotional state affects everyone around you. If you're stressed about a deadline, consider how to acknowledge the pressure without transferring anxiety to your team. You might say, "This deadline is tight, and I want us to deliver quality work without burning out. Let's talk about how to manage this together."

Empathetic Response: When team members share concerns or challenges, your response either builds or erodes trust. Listening without immediately jumping to solutions, acknowledging feelings before addressing facts, and asking "What would be most helpful?" demonstrates empathy.

Rather than imposing new safety rules top-down, Elena asked her construction crew about their biggest safety concerns. She learned that workers often skipped safety protocols because they felt pressure to make up for lost time. "I never want anyone here to choose between their safety and their job," she told the team. "Let's talk about how we can meet our deadlines without cutting corners."

When Trust Breaks: The Art of Repair

Even the most conscientious managers will experience trust breaks—moments when their actions don't align with their words, when mistakes cause harm, or when misunderstandings create distance. The ability to repair trust quickly and effectively often distinguishes great managers from merely good ones.

Trust repair requires a specific sequence of actions that acknowledge the break, take responsibility, and demonstrate commitment to change. This isn't about making excuses or explaining why the trust break wasn't really that bad—it's about owning the impact and rebuilding the foundation.

The Trust Repair Process:

1. **Acknowledge the Break**: Recognize what happened without minimizing or defending. "I realized I didn't follow through on my commitment to

review your project proposal by Friday."

2. **Take Responsibility**: Own your part without blaming external circumstances. "I over-scheduled myself and didn't prioritize this properly."

3. **Express Understanding**: Show you understand the impact on others. "I know this delay affects your timeline and probably creates stress about whether your work is valued."

4. **Make Amends**: Take specific action to address the harm. "I'm reviewing it now and will have feedback to you by end of day today."

5. **Commit to Change**: Explain what you'll do differently going forward. "I'm implementing a better system for tracking commitments so this doesn't happen again."

Kevin's customer service turnaround began with acknowledging past management failures: "I know the previous management style created frustration and broke trust. I can't undo that, but I can commit to a different approach starting now." He followed this with specific behavioral changes and consistent follow-through.

Building Anti-Fragile Trust

The strongest trust isn't just resilient—it's anti-fragile, meaning it gets stronger under stress. Leaders who build anti-fragile trust create relationships that actually benefit from challenges and setbacks. This happens when:

Transparency Increases Under Pressure: Instead of becoming more secretive during difficult times, you become more open about challenges and your thinking process.

Vulnerability Deepens Connections: Admitting when you're uncertain or struggling creates opportunities for team members to support you, strengthening mutual trust.

Shared Problem-Solving Builds Investment: Including the team in addressing trust breaks or other challenges creates joint ownership of solutions.

Learning Becomes Collective: Mistakes become team learning opportunities rather than individual failures, creating a culture where trust grows through shared growth.

Maya's team experienced this when a critical security vulnerability was discovered. Rather than trying to manage the crisis alone, Maya involved the team in both the technical solution and the process improvement: "We need to fix this vulnerability and figure out how to prevent similar issues. Let's work on both together." The crisis became a bonding experience that solidified her leadership credibility.

Real-World Applications: Trust Building in Action

The following extended case studies demonstrate how different managers applied trust-building principles in challenging real-world situations. Each story illustrates the practical application of the frameworks we've discussed while showing the messy, complex reality of building credibility across diverse industries and team dynamics.

Elena's Construction Challenge

Building Trust Through Technical Competence and Safety Leadership

Elena , a 29-year-old structural engineer, became project manager for a large commercial construction site in Phoenix, leading a crew of 15 experienced workers ranging in age from 22 to 58. Most had been in construction for over a decade, while Elena had five years of engineering experience but no management background. The previous manager had left abruptly after a safety incident, creating skepticism about leadership and concerns about job security.

From day one, Elena faced subtle resistance. Workers would look to Marcus, the 52-year-old foreman, for confirmation even after Elena gave clear instructions. During her first team meeting, she noticed side conversations in Spanish (which she speaks fluently but hadn't revealed) where some workers questioned whether "the engineer" understood real construction work.

Elena's trust-building strategy focused on demonstrating competence while showing respect for the crew's experience:

Technical Leadership: Instead of managing from behind a desk, Elena spent mornings reviewing blueprints with the team and afternoons working alongside them. When workers questioned structural modifications, she would physically examine issues together rather than simply citing engineering principles.

Consistent Safety Leadership: Elena implemented predictable daily routines—6:30 AM safety briefings, hourly check-ins during critical operations, and end-of-day updates. When corporate pushed for faster completion, Elena pushed back with data about how safety incidents would cause more delays than careful work.

Transparent Problem-Solving: Rather than imposing new safety rules, Elena asked the crew about their biggest concerns. She learned that workers often skipped protocols due to schedule pressure. "I never want anyone here to choose between their safety and their job," she told them. "Let's figure out how to meet deadlines without cutting corners."

Results: After six weeks, workers began coming directly to Elena with questions instead of routing through Marcus. Safety incidents dropped to zero while productivity increased 12%. When the project completed two days ahead of schedule, several workers requested to stay on Elena's crew for the next phase.

Kevin's Customer Service Recovery

Rebuilding Trust After Inherited Team Demoralization

Kevin inherited a customer service team of 22 representatives after the previous manager was terminated for creating a toxic environment. Employee satisfaction scores were at 2.1 out of 5, customer satisfaction had dropped to 68%, and annual turnover was running at 45%.

The team had learned to avoid initiative rather than risk criticism under the previous punitive management style. Kevin needed to rebuild trust while immediately improving metrics, with only 90 days to show measurable improvement before facing budget cuts.

Kevin's approach focused on trust repair through systems change:

Listening Before Acting: Kevin's first action was scheduling individual 30-minute conversations with each team member, asking what was working, what was frustrating, and what would help them serve customers better.

Quick Wins on Promises: Kevin identified improvements that wouldn't require upper management approval—moving the printer closer to work-stations, upgrading problematic headset equipment, and adjusting break schedules to reduce coverage gaps.

Empowerment Through Recognition: He replaced the previous punishment-focused system with "Solution of the Week" recognition, celebrating representatives who found creative ways to resolve complex customer issues.

Transparent Communication: Kevin shared monthly performance data with the entire team and communicated corporate pressures honestly: "Corporate is pushing for shorter call times, but I've seen how that affects customer satisfaction. I'm advocating for quality metrics that balance efficiency with problem resolution."

Results: By the 90-day mark, customer satisfaction had improved from 68% to 81%, employee satisfaction rose from 2.1 to 3.8, and turnover dropped to 18% annually. Instead of facing budget cuts, the department received additional funding to expand successful programs.

Maya's Startup Identity Crisis

Building Credibility as a Young Leader in a Diverse Team

Maya, a 26-year-old software engineer, was promoted to lead a team of eight developers ranging in age from 23 to 45. The team included both recent coding bootcamp graduates and senior engineers with 15+ years of experience. Several team members were older and more experienced than Maya, including Tom, a 42-year-old senior engineer who had also been considered for the leadership role.

Maya's promotion created subtle tensions, with technical questions still being directed to Tom despite her official leadership role. The startup environment added complexity with aggressive deadlines, changing requirements, and pressure to ship features quickly.

Maya's trust-building approach emphasized competence and humility:

Leading with Technical Strength: When a critical security vulnerability was discovered, Maya dove into the code review personally while coordinating the broader response: "I'm going to work on the authentication module fix while Tom handles the database queries and Sarah works on front-end validation."

Vulnerable Learning: Maya made her learning visible rather than hiding inexperience: "I haven't managed a release this complex before. Tom, based on your experience, what should I be watching for?"

Collaborative Authority: She instituted "failure retrospectives" where the team discussed what went wrong without assigning blame, starting each session by sharing her own mistakes from the week.

Inclusive Process Development: Rather than imposing management processes, Maya worked with the team to develop practices that supported both innovation and coordination.

Results: The security crisis was resolved within 18 hours with no data compromise. Six months later, the team's productivity was 25% higher while code quality scores had improved significantly. When the company needed to create a second development team, Tom specifically requested to continue reporting to Maya rather than lead the new group.

Toolkit: Essential Trust-Building Resources

Trust creates the foundation for every leadership challenge ahead. When people trust your competence, character, and care, they engage in difficult conversations, accept feedback, and work through conflicts constructively.

Quick Reference for This Chapter:

- **Trust Assessment**: See Manager's Toolkit Appendix - Leadership Capability Assessment (Trust section)
- **Trust Repair Conversations**: Use Universal Conversation Framework with trust-specific adaptations
- **Daily Trust Building**: Implement Weekly Leadership Practice Framework (Monday connection check-ins)

Key Takeaways to Practice:

1. **Consistency beats perfection** - small, reliable actions build trust faster than grand gestures
2. **Transparency includes vulnerability** - admitting what you don't know builds rather than undermines credibility
3. **Trust repair follows a predictable process** - acknowledge, take responsibility, commit to change
4. **Cultural sensitivity matters** - adapt your trust-building approach to team members' backgrounds and preferences

This Week's Challenge: Choose one trust-building behavior from the Leadership Capability Assessment where you scored lowest. Practice it daily and notice your team's response.

Credibility comes from consistent, small actions that demonstrate reliability, transparency, and genuine care. Every interaction builds or erodes trust—choose to build it intentionally.

* * *

Next Chapter Preview: In Chapter 6, we'll explore how to master communication and difficult conversations, building on the trust and credibility you've established to have honest, empathetic dialogues that strengthen relationships rather than damage them, even when discussing challenging topics.

6

Mastering Communication and Difficult Conversations

Communication challenges are inevitable when stakes are high or emotions run deep. This chapter provides proven frameworks for meaningful feedback and tough conversations that preserve trust while driving results.

You'll find ready-to-use templates and practical techniques to speak with honesty, show empathy, and make difficult dialogues more productive.

The Psychology of Difficult Conversations

Understanding why conversations feel challenging helps you navigate them more effectively. Our brains perceive confrontation as threat, triggering fight-or-flight responses that can impair rational thinking. Recognizing this biological reality allows you to prepare better and respond more skillfully.

Dr. Douglas Stone, co-author of "Difficult Conversations," identifies three underlying conversations happening simultaneously in any challenging dialogue: the "what happened" conversation (facts and blame), the feelings conversation (emotions and their validity), and the identity conversation (what this says about who we are). Understanding these layers helps managers navigate complexity with greater skill and empathy.

Research by Dr. John Gottman shows that successful difficult conversations share common characteristics: they begin softly, focus on specific behaviors rather than character judgments, include repair attempts when things go wrong, and end with clear agreements about moving forward. For new managers, these insights provide a roadmap for approaching conversations with confidence rather than dread.

The Neuroscience of Feedback Reception

When people receive feedback—especially critical feedback—their brains undergo predictable changes. The anterior cingulate cortex, responsible for processing social pain, activates in ways similar to physical pain. This explains why criticism can literally hurt and why people often become defensive or shut down entirely.

Understanding this neuroscience helps managers frame feedback in ways that minimize threat response and maximize learning. Techniques like starting with strengths, focusing on future improvement rather than past failures, and involving the recipient in problem-solving help keep the prefrontal cortex—the brain's rational center—engaged rather than hijacked by emotional reactivity.

Giving Feedback That Lands

Most new managers hesitate before giving feedback, worrying about damaging working relationships or saying the wrong thing. It's natural to feel concerned about whether someone will take your words to heart—or take them personally.

The key to effective feedback lies in focusing on specific behaviors and their impact rather than making character judgments. This approach, known as the SBI model (Situation-Behavior-Impact), provides a structure that keeps conversations productive and relationship-preserving.

The SBI Framework: Your Foundation for Clear Communication

Situation: Describe the specific context where you observed the behavior

- "In yesterday's client meeting..."
- "During the budget planning session..."
- "When we were reviewing the project timeline..."

Behavior: Describe the observable actions without interpretation or judgment

- "You interrupted the client three times when they were explaining their concerns"
- "The budget numbers you presented didn't include the marketing costs we discussed"
- "You arrived 15 minutes after our scheduled start time"

Impact: Explain the effect of the behavior on outcomes, relationships, or team dynamics

- "This made it difficult for us to understand their real needs and probably left them feeling unheard"
- "Without those costs, our proposal was significantly under budget, which could create problems if we win the contract"
- "We had to backtrack and repeat information, which used up time we needed for decision-making"

Lisa's ICU Application: When nursing supervisor Lisa Chen needed to address medication errors with a team member, she applied SBI carefully: "Over the past month (Situation), I've noticed three instances where medications were administered without the standard double-check protocol being followed (Behavior). These errors could have seriously harmed patients, and I've noticed some colleagues are feeling uncertain about workflow coordination

(Impact)."

The power of SBI lies in its objectivity. By describing what happened rather than why you think it happened, you avoid triggering defensiveness and create space for dialogue about solutions.

Beyond SBI: The Complete Feedback Conversation

While SBI provides the structure for sharing your observations, a complete feedback conversation includes additional elements that build understanding and commitment to change.

Opening with Positive Intent Start by establishing that your goal is support, not punishment:

- "I value our working relationship and want to discuss something that could help us work together even better."
- "I care about your success and want to talk about something I've noticed."

Inviting Their Perspective After sharing your SBI observation, create space for their viewpoint:

- "What's your take on this?"
- "Help me understand your perspective."
- "What factors should I be considering that I might not be aware of?"

This step often reveals crucial context that changes your understanding of the situation entirely.

Collaborative Problem-Solving Rather than prescribing solutions, invite the person to participate in developing them:

- "What ideas do you have for addressing this?"
- "How can I better support you in this area?"

- "What would need to change for this to improve?"

Clear Agreements and Follow-Up End with specific commitments and timeline for checking progress:

- "So we're agreed that you'll... and I'll... Is that right?"
- "When should we follow up on this?"
- "What support do you need from me to make this work?"

The Difficult Conversation Roadmap

When conversations involve conflict, performance issues, or sensitive topics, following a structured approach helps maintain productivity while preserving relationships.

Opening: Start with Positive Intent and Context

The first thirty seconds of a difficult conversation often determine whether it becomes collaborative or adversarial. Your opening should communicate care and establish psychological safety:

"I value our working relationship and want to discuss something that could help us work together even better."

"I've noticed something that I think we should talk about because I care about your success."

Ahmed's Cultural Bridge: When software manager Ahmed needed to address a conflict between team members from different cultural backgrounds, he opened by acknowledging diversity as strength: "We have team members from many different backgrounds, and what feels like helpful communication to one person might feel different to another. That's not anyone's fault—it's something we need to navigate together."

Sharing: Present Your Perspective Using Facts and Impact

Use the SBI framework to share your observations without accusation or interpretation. Avoid inflammatory language and focus on specific examples rather than general patterns.

Tony's Manufacturing Moment: When operations manager Tony needed to address a serious safety violation, he maintained factual focus even when the employee became aggressive: "Yesterday at 3:15 PM during the shift change, you bypassed the lockout system on Line 3 to clear a jam while the machine was still energized. That action put you at risk for serious injury and violates both our safety protocols and OSHA regulations."

Listening: Create Space for Their Perspective

This is often the most challenging part of difficult conversations because it requires genuine curiosity about viewpoints that might contradict your own.

Active Listening Techniques That Work:
Emotional Labeling: "I can hear the frustration in your voice. This seems really important to you."
Clarifying Questions: "When you say 'unfair,' can you help me understand what specifically feels unfair?"
Summarizing: "Let me make sure I understand. You're saying that... Did I get that right?"
Validating: "That makes sense. I can see why you'd feel that way."

Lisa discovered that her nurse's medication errors weren't due to carelessness but exhaustion from working extra shifts to support his family financially. This crucial information only emerged because she created space for his perspective rather than jumping immediately to consequences.

Problem-Solving: Collaborate on Solutions

The most effective solutions emerge from collaborative thinking rather than managerial mandates. When people participate in developing solutions, they're more committed to implementing them.

Effective Problem-Solving Questions:

- "What would need to change for this to improve?"
- "How can I better support you in this area?"
- "What ideas do you have for moving forward?"
- "What obstacles do you anticipate, and how can we address them?"

Closing: Summarize Agreements and Next Steps

End difficult conversations with clarity about what happens next:

- Recap key points and commitments from both parties
- Set specific timelines for follow-up
- Identify what support or resources are needed
- End on a positive, forward-looking note

Managing Emotional Escalation

Even with good preparation and technique, some conversations become emotionally charged. Knowing how to de-escalate tension while maintaining progress toward resolution is a critical skill.

When Someone Becomes Defensive

Defensiveness is a normal response to perceived threat. Rather than pushing through it, acknowledge and address it directly:

Acknowledge Their Reaction: "I can see this is hitting you hard."
Slow Down the Pace: "Let's take a step back for a moment."
Return to Shared Goals: "We both want you to succeed here."
Invite Their Perspective: "What would you like me to understand?"

When You Feel Triggered

Your emotional state affects the entire conversation. When you notice yourself becoming reactive:

Use Internal Grounding Techniques: Take slow breaths, relax your shoulders, remind yourself of your purpose
Buy Time: "That's a good point. Give me a moment to think about that."
Acknowledge Your Reaction: "I'm feeling some strong emotions about this. Let me pause and make sure I'm communicating clearly."
Return to Your Purpose: "What I really want is to find a solution that works for both of us."

Tony applied these techniques when a safety conversation with an experienced worker became heated. Instead of matching the worker's aggressive energy, Tony deliberately lowered his voice and slowed down: "Steve, you've raised some important points. Give me a moment to think about what you're saying." This de-escalation allowed them to address both the safety violation and the underlying production pressures causing stress.

When the Conversation Stalls

Sometimes conversations hit impasses where neither party seems able to move forward:
Normalize the Difficulty: "These conversations aren't easy for anyone."
Try a Different Angle: "Let me approach this differently…"
Take a Break: "Should we pause for a few minutes and come back to this?"
Seek Common Ground: "I think we both agree that…"

Cultural Considerations in Difficult Conversations

Different cultural backgrounds bring varying expectations about directness, hierarchy, emotional expression, and conflict resolution. Effective managers adapt their approach while maintaining authentic communication.

High-Context vs. Low-Context Cultures

High-Context Communication (many Asian, African, and Latin American cultures):

- Pay attention to nonverbal cues and what's not being said
- Allow for indirect communication and face-saving
- Provide more relationship context before addressing issues
- Consider private conversations before group discussions

Low-Context Communication (many Western cultures):

- Be more direct and explicit about issues and expectations
- Focus on facts and specific behaviors
- Address problems quickly and directly
- Separate task feedback from relationship quality

Ahmed navigated this difference when mediating between an American team member who valued direct feedback and an Indian colleague who experienced directness as face-threatening. He adapted his approach to each person's cultural context while helping them understand each other's communication styles.

Power Distance Considerations

High Power Distance (cultures that respect formal hierarchy):

- Show respect for formal roles and seniority
- Allow for more deference in communication
- Provide clear structure and expectations
- Avoid putting people in positions where they might contradict authority publicly

Low Power Distance (cultures that value equality):

- Encourage equal participation regardless of role
- Invite challenges to your perspective
- Collaborate on solutions without emphasizing hierarchy
- Focus on ideas rather than who suggested them

Individual vs. Collective Orientations

Individual-Focused Cultures:

- Emphasize personal growth and achievement
- Address performance issues directly with the individual
- Focus on personal accountability and development

Collective-Focused Cultures:

- Connect feedback to team impact and harmony
- Consider how individual issues affect group dynamics
- Frame solutions in terms of collective benefit

The Courage Challenge: Building Confidence

One effective practice for building confidence is the Courage Challenge. Think ahead to a tough conversation you need to have. Start by writing out your fears—perhaps rejection, losing trust, or not being taken seriously. Next, clarify the ideal outcome: Do you want agreement, better understanding, or a commitment to change?

Courage Challenge Template

The Conversation: What specifically do you need to discuss?
   Your Fears:

   1. _____

      _____

   2. _____

      _____

   3. _____

      _____

Desired Outcomes:

   1. _____

      _____

   2. _____

      _____

Key Messages (3 most important points):

   1. _____

      _____

   2. _____

      _____

3. _____

   _____

Success Measures: How will you know the conversation went well?

Write down the three most important points you need to communicate and phrases you'll use, such as, "My intention here is to support your growth," or "I'd like us to find a way forward together." Define what success looks like—is it mutual understanding, a specific action plan, or simply airing concerns respectfully? Reviewing your plan beforehand boosts confidence and sets you up for a productive exchange.

Post-Conversation Follow-Through

The conversation doesn't end when people leave the room. Effective follow-through is crucial for maintaining momentum and demonstrating commitment to solutions.

Immediate Follow-Up (within 24 hours)

- Send a summary of key points and agreements
- Thank the person for their openness and engagement
- Clarify any remaining questions

* * *

Next Chapter Preview: In Chapter 7, we'll explore how to hire, develop, and retain the talent that will make your team successful, building on the communication skills you've developed to conduct effective interviews, provide meaningful feedback, and create growth opportunities that keep top performers engaged and motivated.

7

Hiring, Developing, and Retaining Talent

Hiring, developing, and keeping great people is a challenge most leaders face at some point. Getting it right can be the difference between building a team that just gets by and one that thrives together over time.

This chapter walks you through finding people with the skills your team needs, making sure everyone gets a fair shot, and helping new hires grow into their roles. You'll learn how to support your team's development through mentoring and training, and how simple acts of recognition can help you keep top talent engaged and motivated.

The Strategic Importance of Talent Management

In today's knowledge economy, the difference between high and low performers can be enormous—research suggests that top performers can be 2-5 times more productive than average performers in complex roles. This performance gap means that hiring, developing, and retaining the right people isn't just an HR function—it's a strategic imperative that directly impacts your team's success.

Dr. Bradford Smart's research on "topgrading" reveals that A-players (top performers) hire other A-players, while B-players often hire C-players to avoid feeling threatened. This creates either a virtuous cycle of excellence or a downward spiral of mediocrity. Your hiring decisions don't just fill immediate needs—they shape your team's future trajectory and culture.

The modern workplace adds complexity to talent management. With remote work, generational diversity, skill obsolescence due to technological change, and increased employee expectations around growth and purpose, managers must be more sophisticated in their approach to building and maintaining strong teams.

The Cost of Poor Hiring Decisions

The financial impact of bad hires is staggering. Conservative estimates suggest that replacing an employee costs 50-200% of their annual salary when you factor in recruitment costs, training time, lost productivity, and team disruption. For managerial roles, the cost can exceed 300% of annual compensation.

But the hidden costs may be even more significant:

- **Team morale impact:** One difficult team member can reduce overall team performance by 30-40%
- **Cultural erosion:** Poor hires can damage psychological safety and team cohesion
- **Manager time drain:** Problem employees require disproportionate management attention
- **Opportunity cost:** Time spent managing performance issues is time not spent on strategic initiatives

Understanding these stakes helps explain why developing strong hiring and development skills is one of the highest-leverage investments a new manager can make.

Building Effective Hiring Processes

Successful hiring combines structured processes with inclusive practices that help you identify the best candidates while building a diverse team.

Defining Core Competencies

Start by identifying the essential skills, behaviors, and characteristics that predict success in the role. Avoid the trap of hiring for "culture fit," which often leads to homogeneous teams and excludes talented people who might bring valuable different perspectives.

Competency Framework Development:
Technical Competencies: The hard skills, knowledge, and experience required to perform the job effectively. Be specific about which technical skills are truly essential versus nice-to-have.
Behavioral Competencies: The soft skills and behavioral patterns that predict success—communication style, problem-solving approach, collaboration ability, and learning agility.
Growth Potential: Indicators that someone can develop and take on increased responsibilities—curiosity, resilience, feedback receptivity, and adaptability.
Values Alignment: Whether someone's core values complement your team culture—integrity, customer focus, quality orientation, or innovation mindset.

Focus on competencies that genuinely predict job performance rather than proxies like specific educational backgrounds or previous company prestige.

Behavioral Interviewing Techniques

Behavioral interviewing, based on the premise that past behavior predicts future performance, provides more reliable hiring decisions than hypothetical questions or culture fit assessments.

STAR Method Framework: Structure behavioral questions to elicit complete responses:

- **Situation:** What was the context?
- **Task:** What needed to be accomplished?
- **Action:** What did the candidate specifically do?
- **Result:** What was the outcome?

Sample Behavioral Questions:

For Problem-Solving: "Tell me about a time when you had to solve a complex problem with limited information. Walk me through your approach."

For Leadership Potential: "Describe a situation where you had to influence someone who didn't report to you to take action. How did you approach it?"

For Learning Agility: "Give me an example of a time you had to quickly learn something completely new. How did you go about it?"

For Resilience: "Tell me about a professional setback you experienced. How did you handle it and what did you learn?"

Follow-up Probes:

- "What would you do differently if you faced that situation again?"
- "How did you measure success in that situation?"
- "What was the most challenging part of that experience?"
- "Who else was involved and how did you work with them?"

Inclusive Hiring Practices

Building diverse teams requires intentional effort to remove barriers and biases from your hiring process.

Job Description Optimization:

- Use gender-neutral language and avoid unnecessary degree requirements

- Focus on essential qualifications rather than exhaustive wish lists
- Include diversity and inclusion statements that feel genuine rather than boilerplate
- Specify which requirements are absolute necessities versus preferences

Bias Reduction Strategies:

- Use structured interviews with consistent questions for all candidates
- Include diverse interview panel members when possible
- Focus on skills-based assessments rather than culture fit evaluations
- Implement blind resume reviews that hide names and graduation dates initially

Candidate Experience Excellence: The hiring process itself becomes a preview of what it's like to work for you and your organization. Every interaction shapes the candidate's perception of your leadership and company culture.

Positive Experience Elements:

- **Clear communication:** Set expectations about timeline and process
- **Respectful scheduling:** Accommodate candidate availability when possible
- **Prompt feedback:** Don't leave candidates hanging
- **Genuine interest:** Ask about their goals and motivations
- **Transparency:** Share realistic job preview, including challenges
- **Professionalism:** Even rejections should be thoughtful and respectful

Remember that candidates are also evaluating you. Top talent has choices, and they're assessing whether they want to work for a manager and organization that values their time and treats them with respect.

Developing Talent and Fostering Growth

Creating a culture where every team member grows begins with well-designed Individual Development Plans (IDPs) and extends to comprehensive support systems that help people reach their potential. The communication skills from Chapter 6 become essential here—you can't effectively develop others without the ability to have honest, constructive conversations about strengths, growth areas, and aspirations.

Individual Development Planning

Collaborative Goal Setting: Work with each team member to identify development goals that align their career aspirations with team needs. The most effective IDPs balance individual interests with organizational requirements.

Development Planning Framework:

1. **Strengths Assessment:** What does this person do exceptionally well?
2. **Growth Areas:** Where do they want to develop new capabilities?
3. **Career Aspirations:** What roles or responsibilities interest them?
4. **Organizational Needs:** How can their development serve team goals?
5. **Resource Identification:** What training, experiences, or support do they need?
6. **Success Metrics:** How will we measure progress?

Types of Development Opportunities:

- **Stretch Assignments:** Projects that require learning new skills
- **Cross-Training:** Exposure to different functions or departments
- **Mentoring:** Both receiving guidance and mentoring others
- **Conference Attendance:** External learning and networking opportunities
- **Skills Training:** Formal education or certification programs

- **Leadership Opportunities:** Chances to lead projects or initiatives

Mentorship and Sponsorship

Understanding the difference between mentorship and sponsorship helps you provide the right type of support for different team members at different career stages.

Mentorship involves sharing knowledge, providing guidance, and supporting skill development. Mentors help people learn, navigate challenges, and make good decisions.

Sponsorship involves advocating for someone's advancement, providing access to opportunities, and using your influence to support their career progression. Sponsors open doors and create visibility for high-potential team members.

Effective Mentoring Practices:

- Meet regularly and consistently
- Focus on the mentee's agenda and goals
- Share experiences and lessons learned
- Ask powerful questions that promote reflection
- Provide honest feedback and challenge thinking
- Connect mentees with additional resources and people

Sponsorship Opportunities:

- Recommend team members for high-visibility projects
- Include them in strategic meetings and decisions
- Advocate for their promotion or advancement
- Connect them with senior leaders and influencers
- Share their achievements with broader networks

Recognition and Performance Feedback

Consistent recognition and development-focused feedback create conditions where people feel valued and motivated to grow.

Effective Recognition Principles:

- **Specific:** Describe exactly what the person did well
- **Timely:** Provide recognition close to when the achievement occurred
- **Personal:** Tailor recognition to what motivates each individual
- **Public:** Share achievements with others when appropriate
- **Meaningful:** Connect recognition to larger goals and values

Development-Focused Feedback Framework: Use the SBI model from Chapter 6, enhanced with development focus:

- **Situation:** Context for the feedback
- **Behavior:** What you observed
- **Impact:** Effect on results and others
- **Development:** Growth opportunities and next steps

Regular Feedback Rhythms:

- **Weekly check-ins:** Brief conversations about progress and obstacles
- **Monthly development discussions:** Deeper conversations about growth and career goals
- **Quarterly formal reviews:** Comprehensive assessment of performance and development progress
- **Annual planning sessions:** Setting goals and development priorities for the coming year

Retention Strategies

Keeping top talent requires understanding what motivates different people and creating conditions where they feel engaged, challenged, and valued.

Understanding Retention Drivers

Research consistently shows that people leave managers, not companies. The top retention drivers include:

Growth Opportunities: People want to develop new skills and advance their careers

Recognition: Feeling valued and appreciated for contributions

Autonomy: Having control over how work gets done

Purpose: Understanding how their work contributes to something meaningful

Relationships: Positive connections with colleagues and managers

Work-Life Integration: Flexibility and support for personal priorities

Proactive Retention Practices

Career Pathing: Help people see potential futures within the organization, even if they're not linear promotion paths.

Skills Investment: Provide training, conference attendance, and other development opportunities that make people more valuable (and more committed).

Flexibility Options: Where possible, offer flexible schedules, remote work, or other arrangements that improve work-life integration.

Team Building: Create opportunities for genuine relationship-building among team members.

Open Communication: Maintain an environment where people feel safe raising concerns before they become resignation triggers.

Case Study Integration: Lisa's Healthcare Development Program

Lisa, a 34-year-old nursing supervisor at a regional hospital, faced a retention crisis when three experienced nurses left in six months, citing lack of growth opportunities and feeling undervalued.

The Challenge: Healthcare organizations often struggle with retention due to high stress, demanding schedules, and limited advancement paths. Lisa's unit had a 35% annual turnover rate—well above industry averages.

Development Strategy Implementation:

Individual Career Conversations: Lisa scheduled one-on-one meetings with each nurse to understand their career goals and frustrations. She discovered that many felt stuck in their current roles with no clear path forward.

Skills-Based Development Tracks: Working with hospital administration, Lisa created three development tracks:

- **Clinical Expertise:** Advanced certifications and specialization opportunities
- **Leadership Development:** Mentoring and supervisory skill building
- **Education and Training:** Opportunities to teach and develop others

Mentorship Program: Lisa paired experienced nurses with newer staff, creating both development opportunities for mentees and leadership experience for mentors.

Recognition System: She implemented weekly "care impact" stories where nurses shared examples of how they made a difference in patient outcomes.

Flexible Scheduling: Lisa advocated successfully for more flexible scheduling options that accommodated continuing education and family commitments.

Results:

- Turnover dropped to 18% within eight months
- Patient satisfaction scores increased 12%
- Three nurses completed advanced certifications

- Two nurses were promoted to leadership roles in other units
- Unit was recognized as "exemplary" by hospital administration

Key Learning: Lisa discovered that retention isn't just about compensation—it's about creating pathways for growth, recognition, and meaningful contribution. When people can see a future for themselves and feel valued in the present, they're much more likely to stay engaged and committed.

By integrating structured hiring processes, development-focused mentoring, consistent recognition practices, and proactive retention strategies, you create an environment where every employee feels seen, supported, and motivated to achieve their fullest potential.

The investment you make in your people's growth and satisfaction pays dividends not just in performance and retention, but in your own development as a leader. There's profound satisfaction in watching someone you've mentored succeed, seeing skills you've helped develop create new opportunities, and knowing that your leadership has made a positive difference in people's careers and lives.

This Week's Challenge

Conduct a talent management assessment for your team:

1. **Review your hiring process** for potential bias and effectiveness gaps
2. **Schedule development conversations** with each team member about their career goals
3. **Identify one person** ready for a stretch assignment or new opportunity
4. **Create a recognition plan** that acknowledges different types of contributions
5. **Assess retention risks** and develop specific strategies for your highest-value team members

* * *

Next Chapter Preview: In Chapter 8, we'll explore how the hiring, development, and retention work connects to creating inclusive, high-trust team cultures where everyone can bring their best selves to work.

8

Building Inclusive, High-Trust Team Cultures

Creating a team culture where everyone feels valued and trusted doesn't happen overnight. It's built through daily choices, small actions, and the willingness to have honest conversations about what inclusion really means in practice.

This chapter explores how to foster psychological safety, address bias thoughtfully, and build rituals that bring out the best in every team member. You'll find practical strategies for making inclusion more than a buzzword and creating environments where diverse perspectives strengthen rather than divide your team.

The Business Case for Inclusive Cultures

Research consistently demonstrates that inclusive teams significantly outperform homogeneous ones across multiple metrics that directly impact business results.

McKinsey's extensive research on diversity shows that companies in the top quartile for ethnic diversity are 36% more likely to outperform their peers financially, while those in the top quartile for gender diversity are 25% more likely to achieve above-average profitability. But these benefits don't emerge simply from having diverse representation—they require inclusive cultures where different perspectives are genuinely valued and leveraged.

Dr. Scott Page's research at the University of Michigan reveals that diverse teams consistently outperform homogeneous teams of high-ability individuals when tackling complex problems. The key insight is that diversity of thought, experience, and perspective provides "cognitive diversity" that enhances problem-solving and innovation. However, this advantage only materializes in environments with high psychological safety and trust.

The Psychological Safety Foundation

Google's Project Aristotle, which analyzed hundreds of teams to identify what makes them effective, found that psychological safety was the single most important factor in team performance. Teams with high psychological safety had significantly better outcomes in terms of innovation, error reduction, and overall effectiveness.

Amy Edmondson defines psychological safety as "a belief that one can speak up without risk of punishment or humiliation." In psychologically safe environments, people feel confident to admit mistakes, ask questions, propose ideas, and challenge the status quo without fear of negative consequences.

For new managers, understanding that psychological safety is measurable and buildable—not just a nice-to-have cultural element—provides a concrete framework for creating the conditions where inclusion can flourish.

Fostering Psychological Safety

Creating psychological safety requires intentional effort and consistent modeling from leadership.

Leadership Behaviors That Build Safety

Admit Your Own Mistakes: When you acknowledge errors openly and discuss what you learned, you demonstrate that mistakes are learning opportunities rather than failures.

Ask for Feedback: Regularly seek input about your own performance and decisions. This shows that questioning and improvement are valued.

Model Curiosity: When someone shares a different perspective, respond with genuine questions rather than immediate judgment or correction.

Respond to Failure Constructively: When team members make mistakes, focus on understanding what happened and how to prevent similar issues rather than assigning blame.

Celebrate Learning: Recognize team members who try new approaches, even when they don't work perfectly.

Creating Safe Spaces for Difficult Conversations

Regular Team Retrospectives: Schedule time for the team to discuss what's working well and what could be improved, both in processes and relation-ships.

Anonymous Feedback Channels: Provide ways for people to share concerns or suggestions without attribution when needed.

Conflict Resolution Support: When tensions arise between team members, offer to facilitate conversations rather than hoping issues resolve themselves.

Bias Interruption: When you notice exclusionary behavior, address it promptly and directly while maintaining respect for all involved.

Carlos's Manufacturing Inclusion

Carlos, a 41-year-old plant supervisor at a manufacturing facility, inherited a team with a history of discrimination complaints and low morale among diverse workers.

The Challenge: The manufacturing environment had a deeply ingrained culture of "fitting in" that often excluded women, minorities, and younger workers. Several talented employees had transferred to other departments or left the company entirely.

Building Psychological Safety:

Listen First: Carlos started by conducting confidential one-on-one conversations with every team member to understand their experiences and concerns without making immediate judgments or promises.

Acknowledge the Problem: In a team meeting, he acknowledged the history of exclusionary behavior and committed to creating a more inclusive environment where everyone could contribute effectively.

Establish New Norms: Working with the team, Carlos developed explicit guidelines for respectful communication, decision-making processes that included diverse perspectives, and consequences for exclusionary behavior.

Model Vulnerability: Carlos shared his own learning process, admitting when he didn't understand cultural differences and asking team members to help educate him.

Address Issues Directly: When exclusionary behavior occurred, Carlos addressed it immediately through private conversations, focusing on behavior change rather than character attacks.

Results:

- Discrimination complaints dropped to zero within six months
- Team productivity increased 15% as previously marginalized workers became more engaged
- Two women and one Latino worker were promoted to lead positions
- The plant became a model for other facilities in the company

Key Learning: Carlos discovered that psychological safety requires both visible leadership commitment and systematic behavior change. People needed to see consistent action over time before they trusted that the culture was genuinely changing.

Recognizing and Addressing Bias

Everyone has unconscious biases—mental shortcuts our brains use to process information quickly. The goal isn't to eliminate bias (which is impossible) but to recognize it and prevent it from negatively affecting team dynamics and decisions.

Types of Workplace Bias

Affinity Bias: Preferring people who are similar to us in background, interests, or communication style.

Confirmation Bias: Seeking information that confirms our existing beliefs while ignoring contradictory evidence.

Attribution Bias: Making assumptions about why people behave in certain ways based on limited information.

Halo Effect: Letting one positive characteristic influence our overall judgment of someone.

Horns Effect: Letting one negative characteristic overshadow other qualities.

Recency Bias: Overweighting recent events when making decisions about performance or capability.

Bias Interruption Strategies

Pause and Reflect: When making decisions about people, take time to consider whether bias might be influencing your judgment.

Seek Diverse Input: Include different perspectives in hiring, promotion, and project assignment decisions.

Use Structured Processes: Implement consistent criteria and evaluation methods that reduce the influence of subjective impressions.

Question Your Assumptions: When you notice yourself making judgments about someone's capabilities or motivations, explore whether you have sufficient evidence.

Address Bias When You See It: When you observe exclusionary behavior, address it constructively: "I noticed that Maria's idea was interrupted. Let's give her a chance to finish her thought."

Building Inclusive Rituals and Practices

Sustainable inclusion requires embedding inclusive practices into the regular rhythms of team life. These rituals and practices help maintain focus on inclusion even during busy periods and create consistent experiences that build trust over time.

Team Rituals That Build Connection

Personal Story Sharing: Monthly sessions where team members share something meaningful about their background, interests, or experiences. This builds empathy and understanding.

Failure Celebrations: Quarterly sessions where people share mistakes they made and lessons learned, normalizing vulnerability and learning.

Strength Spotlights: Regular opportunities for team members to recognize each other's contributions and unique capabilities.

Cultural Sharing: Rotating opportunities for team members to share aspects of their cultural backgrounds, holidays, or traditions.

Innovation Time: Dedicated time for people to work on projects they're passionate about, regardless of their direct work relevance.

Inclusive Meeting Practices

Pre-meeting Preparation: Share agendas in advance and invite input on topics, ensuring everyone can prepare to contribute.

Rotation of Roles: Have different people facilitate meetings, take notes, and present updates to develop skills and share visibility.

Think-Pair-Share: Use structured discussion formats that give everyone time to formulate thoughts before sharing with the group.

Silent Brainstorming: Include individual reflection time before group discussions to ensure quieter voices have space to contribute.

Meeting Equity Check: Regularly assess whether speaking time and idea adoption are distributed fairly across team members.

Rachel's Remote Culture Building

Rachel, a 32-year-old marketing manager, faced the challenge of building inclusive culture across a distributed team that had never worked together in person.

   The Challenge: Building trust and inclusion without face-to-face interaction required creativity and intentional relationship-building activities that worked across different time zones and cultural backgrounds.

Virtual Culture Building:

Weekly Culture Moments: Rachel started each team meeting with a 5-minute cultural sharing where someone talked about a tradition, holiday, or personal interest from their background.

Digital Coffee Chats: She facilitated rotating small-group video calls where team members could have informal conversations outside of work topics.

Collaborative Playlist: The team created a shared music playlist where everyone contributed songs meaningful to them, creating conversations about different musical traditions and personal stories.

Virtual Lunch-and-Learns: Monthly sessions where team members taught each other skills—both professional (like design techniques) and personal (like cooking traditional foods).

Inclusive Decision-Making: Rachel implemented asynchronous decision-making processes that gave everyone time to contribute regardless of communication style or time zone.

Recognition Rituals: She created a weekly "wins and appreciation" document where team members could recognize each other's contributions and celebrate successes.

Results:

- Team engagement scores ranked in the top 10% company-wide despite being fully remote
- Cross-cultural collaboration increased, with team members regularly working across geographic boundaries
- Three team members were promoted, with colleagues from different continents serving as references
- The team's inclusive practices were adopted by other departments

Key Learning: Rachel discovered that inclusion in remote environments requires even more intentionality than in-person teams, but the results can be stronger because every interaction must be purposeful and thoughtful.

Measuring Inclusion Progress

Like any important business objective, inclusion efforts should be measured and tracked over time. This helps identify progress and areas that need attention.

Inclusion Metrics to Track

Participation Metrics:

- Speaking time distribution in meetings
- Idea adoption rates across different team members
- Development opportunity participation
- Feedback quality and frequency

Experience Metrics:

- Retention rates across different groups
- Promotion and advancement patterns
- Survey responses about sense of belonging
- Exit interview feedback about inclusive culture

Behavioral Metrics:

- Frequency of bias interruption
- Cross-cultural collaboration instances
- Informal relationship building across differences
- Conflict resolution success rates

Creating Feedback Loops

Regular Pulse Surveys: Brief monthly surveys asking about inclusion experiences and belonging

Focus Groups: Quarterly discussions with different demographic groups about their experiences and suggestions.

Anonymous Feedback Channels: Always-available ways for people to share concerns or suggestions about inclusion.

Leadership 360 Assessments: Include inclusion competencies in management evaluation processes.

Building inclusive, high-trust team cultures is ongoing work that requires consistent attention and commitment. It's not a destination but a journey of continuous learning and improvement. The effort invested in creating psychological safety, addressing bias, and building inclusive practices pays dividends in team performance, innovation, and individual satisfaction.

The foundation you're building here—where every team member feels valued, heard, and able to contribute their best work—becomes the platform for navigating the complexities of remote work, conflict resolution, and strategic challenges that we'll explore in the coming chapters.

This Week's Challenge

Implement one inclusive practice this week:

1. **Conduct a team inclusion audit** using the metrics from this chapter

2. **Introduce one new inclusive meeting practice** (like silent brainstorming or role rotation)
3. **Have a psychological safety conversation** with your team about what makes them feel safe to speak up
4. **Address one instance of bias** you observe in team interactions
5. **Start one team ritual** that builds connection and understanding across differences

* * *

Next Chapter Preview: In Chapter 9, we'll explore how to maintain the inclusive culture you've been building when managing remote and hybrid teams across screens and time zones.

III

Part III: Leading Through Complex Challenges

Advanced leadership challenges

Navigate the sophisticated leadership situations that separate good managers from great ones—managing distributed teams, resolving conflicts, thinking strategically, and leading through crisis with confidence and clarity.

9

Managing Remote and Hybrid Teams

Managing people you can't always see in person brings its own set of challenges and opportunities. Building trust across screens, keeping everyone connected, and making sure no one gets left out requires intentional effort and new approaches to leadership.

This chapter covers practical strategies for creating strong remote team cultures, managing performance when you can't observe daily work, and making sure hybrid arrangements work for everyone. You'll find specific tools for virtual communication, team building, and maintaining the inclusive culture you've been developing.

The New Reality of Distributed Work

The shift to remote and hybrid work isn't just a temporary accommodation— it's a fundamental change in how work gets done. Research from MIT shows that remote work has increased productivity by 13-50% in many knowledge work roles, while simultaneously reducing commute times, office costs, and geographic barriers to talent. However, these benefits only materialize when remote work is managed intentionally and skillfully.

The Stanford Work From Home Study found that while productivity increased, promotion rates decreased for remote workers. This suggests that while people can do their current jobs effectively from home, career advancement requires additional attention in distributed environments.

For new managers, this presents both opportunity and challenge. You have access to talent pools that weren't previously available, greater flexibility in how work gets done, and the potential for improved work-life integration for your team. However, you also need to develop new skills for building relationships, managing performance, and maintaining culture without the benefit of spontaneous in-person interactions.

The Psychological Challenges of Remote Work

Remote work creates unique psychological challenges that managers must understand and address:

Isolation and Loneliness: Even introverted team members can experience loneliness when working remotely. The casual interactions that happen naturally in offices disappear in remote settings.

Blurred Boundaries: When home becomes office, many people struggle to separate work and personal life, leading to overwork or difficulty focusing.

Communication Overload: The absence of nonverbal cues leads to more written communication, which can feel overwhelming and create misunderstandings.

Visibility Anxiety: Team members may worry about being "out of sight, out of mind" when it comes to recognition, development opportunities, and career advancement.

Technology Fatigue: Constant video calls and digital collaboration can be mentally exhausting in ways that in-person interaction isn't.

Understanding these challenges helps managers proactively address them rather than simply reacting when problems arise.

Communication Excellence in Remote Settings

Effective remote communication requires more structure and intentionality than in-person interaction. The casual conversations and nonverbal cues that facilitate understanding in offices must be replaced with deliberate communication practices.

Establishing Communication Protocols

Tool Selection and Usage Guidelines:
Instant Messaging: Use for quick questions, informal updates, and non-urgent coordination. Expected response time within a few hours during working time.
Email: Use for formal communications, external stakeholders, and information that needs documentation. Expected response time within 24-48 hours.
Video Calls: Use for complex discussions, relationship building, and sensitive conversations. Schedule in advance with clear agendas.
Phone Calls: Use for urgent issues, quick decision-making, or when other tools aren't working. Follow up with written summary of key points.

Over-Communication Strategies

Remote work requires more communication than in-person work because you can't rely on visual cues to understand how people are doing or what challenges they're facing.

Daily Communication Rhythms:

- **Morning check-ins:** Brief updates on priorities and any obstacles
- **Midday progress shares:** Quick status updates on key projects
- **End-of-day summaries:** Accomplishments and plans for tomorrow

Weekly Communication Structure:

- **Team meetings:** Focus on coordination and collective problem-solving
- **One-on-ones:** Individual development and relationship building
- **Project reviews:** Detailed progress assessment and course correction

Managing Across Time Zones

When team members work across different time zones, communication becomes even more complex but also more important for maintaining connection and coordination.

Asynchronous Communication Best Practices:

- **Comprehensive written updates:** Provide enough detail that people can understand context without follow-up questions
- **Decision documentation:** Record rationale and next steps so people can stay informed
- **Video recordings:** Use tools like Loom to explain complex concepts when live discussion isn't possible
- **Threaded conversations:** Use platforms that maintain context and allow people to catch up efficiently

Synchronous Meeting Optimization:

- **Rotate meeting times:** Share the inconvenience of early/late meetings across team members
- **Record important sessions:** Allow people to catch up if they can't attend live
- **Focus on high-value interactions:** Use synchronous time for relationship building and complex problem-solving

Building Remote Team Culture

Creating strong team culture remotely requires replacing the spontaneous interactions of office life with intentional relationship-building activities.

Virtual Team Building Strategies

Regular Social Connections:

- **Virtual coffee chats:** Informal 15-minute conversations between team members
- **Online lunch sessions:** Shared meal times where people can connect personally
- **Digital happy hours:** Casual end-of-week gatherings with no work agenda
- **Team trivia or games:** Lighthearted competitions that build camaraderie

Shared Experiences:

- **Book clubs:** Reading and discussing the same book together
- **Skill sharing:** Team members teaching each other professional or personal skills
- **Collaborative playlists:** Music sharing that reveals personal tastes and cultural backgrounds
- **Photo challenges:** Weekly themes where people share pictures related to their lives

Recognition and Celebration:

- **Digital praise walls:** Shared spaces where team members can recognize each other's contributions
- **Virtual milestone celebrations:** Online parties for birthdays, work anniversaries, and achievements

- **Team challenges:** Collective goals like steps walked, books read, or volunteer hours contributed
- **Seasonal celebrations:** Adapted holiday parties and special occasion acknowledgments

Michael's Hybrid Healthcare System

Michael, a 44-year-old healthcare administrator, managed a team split between remote administrative staff and on-site clinical workers, creating unique challenges around fairness and communication.

The Challenge: Maintaining equity between remote and in-person workers while ensuring both groups felt valued and included in team culture and decision-making.

Hybrid Management Strategy:

Communication Equity: Michael established protocols ensuring that all important information was shared digitally, even when some team members were physically present. In-person hallway conversations were documented and shared with remote workers.

Meeting Inclusion: All meetings were conducted via video conference, even when some participants were in the same building. This ensured remote workers had equal participation opportunities.

Professional Development: Development opportunities were distributed fairly between remote and on-site workers, with some training conducted virtually to include everyone.

Performance Standards: Michael created outcome-based performance metrics that worked equally well for remote and in-person workers, focusing on results rather than activities.

Social Connection: He organized monthly hybrid social events—some virtual, some in-person with virtual participation options—ensuring both groups could build relationships.

Career Advancement: Michael made promotion and advancement decisions based on performance and potential, not physical presence, actively counteracting proximity bias.

Results:

- Employee satisfaction scores remained consistent between remote and on-site workers
- Productivity improved 22% as the team leveraged the advantages of both work arrangements
- Zero turnover related to work arrangement preferences
- The hybrid model was adopted as best practice across the healthcare system

Key Learning: Michael discovered that successful hybrid management requires explicit policies and processes to ensure equity. Without intentional effort, proximity bias naturally advantages in-person workers.

Performance Management in Distributed Teams

Managing performance when you can't observe daily work requires shifting from activity-based to results-based management approaches.

Results-Oriented Performance Systems

Clear Outcome Definition: Instead of tracking hours or activities, focus on specific, measurable outcomes that contribute to team and organizational goals.

SMART-R Goal Framework:

- **Specific:** Clearly defined outcomes
- **Measurable:** Quantifiable success metrics
- **Achievable:** Realistic given resources and constraints
- **Relevant:** Connected to team and organizational priorities
- **Time-bound:** Clear deadlines and milestones

- **Reviewed:** Regular check-ins and adjustments

Performance Indicators:

- **Quality Metrics:** Standards for work output and accuracy
- **Timeline Adherence:** Meeting deadlines and project milestones
- **Collaboration Effectiveness:** How well they work with others
- **Initiative and Innovation:** Going beyond basic requirements
- **Communication Quality:** Clarity and responsiveness in interactions

Regular Check-ins and Feedback

Weekly One-on-Ones Structure:

- **Progress Review (10 minutes):** What was accomplished and any obstacles encountered
- **Support Needs (5 minutes):** Resources, help, or clarification required
- **Relationship Building (10 minutes):** Personal connection and team dynamics
- **Forward Planning (5 minutes):** Priorities for the coming week

Monthly Development Conversations:

- **Goal Progress Assessment:** Review advancement toward development and performance goals
- **Skill Development:** Discuss learning opportunities and growth areas
- **Career Conversations:** Explore long-term aspirations and pathways
- **Feedback Exchange:** Both manager and team member share observations and suggestions

Building Accountability Without Micromanagement

Remote work requires trust-based accountability systems that focus on results while providing support when needed.

Accountability Strategies:
Transparent Progress Tracking: Use shared dashboards or documents where team members update their progress regularly. This creates visibility without requiring constant check-ins.
Peer Accountability: Pair team members for mutual accountability and support. This distributes accountability beyond just the manager-employee relationship.
Regular Milestone Reviews: Break large projects into smaller milestones with regular review points. This allows for course correction without waiting for final deliverables.
Self-Assessment Practices: Have team members regularly assess their own performance and identify areas where they need support or development.
Resource Accessibility: Ensure people have easy access to the tools, information, and support they need to be successful.

Addressing Performance Issues Remotely

When performance issues arise in remote environments, they must be addressed quickly and directly. The lack of casual interaction means problems can persist longer without manager awareness.

Early Intervention Framework:
Pattern Recognition: Look for changes in communication frequency, quality of work, meeting participation, or collaboration patterns.
Direct Conversation: Address concerns promptly through video calls rather than written communication for sensitive topics.
Root Cause Analysis: Explore whether performance issues stem from technical problems, personal challenges, unclear expectations, or skill gaps.

Collaborative Problem-Solving: Work together to identify solutions and support systems that can help improve performance.

Follow-up Systems: Establish more frequent check-ins and clear success metrics for improvement.

Hybrid Work Challenges and Solutions

Hybrid work—where some team members work remotely while others are in the office—presents unique challenges around fairness, communication, and culture. The goal is to create equity of experience regardless of where people work.

Avoiding the Two-Class System

One of the biggest risks in hybrid environments is creating a system where in-office workers have advantages over remote workers in terms of information access, relationship building, and career opportunities.

Equity Strategies:

Default to Digital: Even when some people are in the same physical location, conduct meetings and share information through digital channels that remote workers can access equally.

Information Sharing Protocols: Ensure that hallway conversations and informal discussions are documented and shared with remote team members.

Meeting Participation Standards: Use video conferencing for all meetings, even when some participants are co-located, to ensure equal participation opportunities.

Development Equity: Distribute training, mentoring, and advancement opportunities fairly between remote and in-person workers.

Performance Evaluation: Base assessments on outcomes and contributions rather than physical presence or visibility.

Zara's Global Software Team

Zara, a 30-year-old product manager, led a software development team distributed across four continents, requiring coordination across time zones and cultural differences.

The Challenge: Coordinating work across 16-hour time zone differences while maintaining team cohesion and ensuring all voices were heard in product decisions.

Global Team Management:

Asynchronous-First Workflow: Zara designed processes that worked asynchronously, using synchronous meetings only for relationship building and complex problem-solving that required real-time interaction.

Cultural Bridge Building: She invested time in understanding cultural communication styles and work preferences, adapting her management approach for different team members while maintaining consistent standards.

Documentation Excellence: All decisions, rationale, and next steps were documented comprehensively so team members could stay informed regardless of when they were online.

Rotating Leadership: Different team members led meetings and initiatives based on their time zones and expertise, distributing leadership across the global team.

Strategic Synchronous Time: Zara identified core overlap hours and used them efficiently for high-value collaborative work like design sessions and problem-solving discussions.

Cultural Learning Initiatives: The team held monthly cultural sharing sessions where members taught others about their work styles, holidays, and communication preferences.

Results:

- Successfully launched three major product features with 98% on-time delivery
- Team satisfaction scores ranked in the top 5% globally within the

company
- Zero cultural conflict incidents despite diverse backgrounds
- Two team members were promoted to lead their own global teams
- The team's collaboration model was adopted company-wide for international projects

Key Learning: Zara discovered that managing global teams requires designing for the most constrained situation (the person in the most challenging time zone) and building cultural competence as a core leadership skill.

Technology and Tools for Remote Success

Effective remote management requires mastering the tools and technologies that enable distributed work. The right technology stack can significantly improve communication, collaboration, and productivity.

Essential Remote Management Tools

Communication Platforms:

- **Instant Messaging:** Tools like Slack, Microsoft Teams, or Discord for quick communication and team channels
- **Video Conferencing:** Platforms like Zoom, Google Meet, or Microsoft Teams for face-to-face interaction
- **Asynchronous Video:** Tools like Loom or Vidyard for sharing updates or explanations that can be viewed on demand

Collaboration Tools:

- **Document Sharing:** Google Workspace, Microsoft 365, or similar platforms for real-time document collaboration
- **Project Management:** Tools like Asana, Trello, or Monday.com for tracking work and deadlines

- **Virtual Whiteboards:** Platforms like Miro, Figma, or Mural for visual collaboration and brainstorming

Productivity Systems:

- **Time Management:** Tools like RescueTime or Toggl for understanding how time is spent
- **Focus Support:** Apps like Freedom or Cold Turkey to manage distractions
- **Workflow Automation:** Tools like Zapier or Microsoft Power Automate to streamline routine tasks

Security and Privacy Considerations

Remote work introduces security vulnerabilities that managers must address to protect both company information and employee privacy.

Remote Security Best Practices:

Device Management: Ensure team members have secure, updated devices with appropriate security software.

Network Security: Provide guidance on secure internet connections and VPN usage when handling sensitive information.

Data Protection: Establish clear protocols for handling, storing, and sharing confidential information in remote environments.

Privacy Boundaries: Respect the boundary between work and personal space when conducting video calls or requesting access to personal devices.

Backup Systems: Ensure important work and data are backed up regularly and accessible if personal equipment fails.

Future of Remote and Hybrid Work

The distributed work trend will likely continue evolving, requiring managers to stay adaptable and continue developing their remote leadership capabilities.

Emerging Trends and Considerations

Increased Flexibility Expectations: Employees increasingly expect flexible work arrangements as a standard benefit rather than a special accommodation.

Global Talent Access: Organizations are expanding their talent pools globally, requiring managers to develop cross-cultural competence.

Technology Evolution: New tools and platforms will continue emerging to better support distributed collaboration and relationship building.

Workspace Redesign: Physical offices are being redesigned to support collaboration and connection rather than individual work.

Well-being Focus: Organizations are recognizing the need to actively support employee mental health and work-life integration in remote environments.

The trust-building, communication, and inclusive culture work from previous chapters becomes even more critical when managing across screens and time zones. The investment you make in creating strong remote team cultures pays dividends in productivity, employee satisfaction, and your ability to access broader talent pools.

Your success as a remote manager isn't measured by how well you replicate in-person experiences virtually, but by how effectively you create new forms of connection, accountability, and collaboration that leverage the unique advantages of distributed work.

This Week's Challenge

Optimize your remote/hybrid management approach:

1. **Audit your communication tools and protocols** to ensure they serve your team effectively
2. **Implement one new practice** that builds connection across your distributed team
3. **Review performance management** to ensure it focuses on outcomes

rather than activities

4. **Address any equity gaps** between remote and in-person team members
5. **Schedule individual conversations** with team members about their remote work experience and needs

* * *

Next Chapter Preview: In Chapter 10, we'll explore how to navigate conflict and challenging situations, building on the remote and hybrid management skills you've developed to address disagreements constructively, manage difficult personalities, and turn team tensions into opportunities for stronger collaboration and trust.

10

Navigating Conflict and Challenging Situations

Conflict is inevitable in any workplace where people care about outcomes and have different perspectives on how to achieve them. The difference between teams that thrive and those that struggle often comes down to how effectively they navigate disagreement and tension. Many new managers avoid conflict, hoping problems will resolve themselves, or handle it poorly, creating lasting damage to relationships and team effectiveness.

Effective conflict management isn't about eliminating disagreement—it's about channeling different perspectives into productive collaboration. This chapter provides frameworks for understanding conflict dynamics, de-escalating tense situations, and building teams that handle disagreement constructively.

Understanding the Conflict Spectrum

Not all workplace tensions require the same response. Understanding where conflicts fall on the spectrum helps you choose appropriate intervention strategies.

Task Conflict focuses on work-related disagreements—different approaches to solving problems, resource allocation decisions, or priority setting. This type of conflict can actually improve outcomes when managed well, as diverse perspectives lead to better solutions.

Process Conflict involves disagreements about how work gets done—meeting formats, communication protocols, or decision-making procedures. These conflicts often seem minor but can significantly impact team efficiency if left unresolved.

Relationship Conflict centers on personal tensions between individuals—personality clashes, trust issues, or communication style differences. This type of conflict typically hurts team performance and requires careful intervention.

Status Conflict emerges from disputes about roles, authority, or recognition—who makes certain decisions, whose ideas get credit, or how influence is distributed. These conflicts can be particularly challenging because they touch on fundamental human needs for respect and autonomy.

Conflict Escalation Patterns

Most workplace conflicts follow predictable escalation patterns. Recognizing these stages helps you intervene before situations become destructive.

Stage 1: Differences - People notice they have different perspectives but assume good intent and work toward understanding.

Stage 2: Disagreement - Differences become more pronounced and people begin advocating more strongly for their positions.

Stage 3: Competition - Individuals start viewing the situation as win-lose and focus on proving their position is correct.

Stage 4: Campaign - People seek allies and build coalitions to support their perspective, often involving others unnecessarily.

Stage 5: Litigation - The conflict becomes about being right rather than solving problems, with formal complaints or escalation to authority figures.

The goal is to address conflicts in Stages 1-2 before they escalate to later stages where resolution becomes much more difficult.

The CALM Method for Conflict Resolution

When facing active conflict, the CALM method provides a systematic approach for productive resolution:

C - Center Yourself Before engaging in conflict resolution, manage your own emotional state. Take time to breathe, identify your triggers, and approach the situation with genuine curiosity rather than defensiveness.

A - Acknowledge All Perspectives Ensure everyone feels heard before moving toward solutions. This doesn't mean agreeing with all viewpoints, but rather demonstrating that you understand what each person values and why they hold their position.

L - Listen for Underlying Interests Look beyond stated positions to understand underlying needs and concerns. Often what people ask for isn't what they actually need, and creative solutions become possible when you address root interests.

M - Manage Toward Solutions Focus the conversation on finding mutually acceptable outcomes rather than determining who was right or wrong. Emphasize shared goals and collaborative problem-solving.

Applying CALM in Practice

Samantha's experience with generational conflict demonstrates how this method works in real situations. When veteran designers clashed with younger team members over creative approaches, she used CALM to bridge seemingly incompatible perspectives.

Centering: Rather than choosing sides immediately, Samantha took time to understand the deeper dynamics at play and planned her intervention thoughtfully.

Acknowledging: She validated both groups' concerns—veterans' desire to maintain quality standards and newcomers' need to contribute innovative ideas.

Listening: Through careful questioning, she discovered that both groups shared the same ultimate goal of creating outstanding work for clients, despite their different approaches.

Managing: She created structures that leveraged each group's strengths— reverse mentoring programs and innovation hours that turned competition into collaboration.

De-escalation Techniques

When emotions run high, your first priority is reducing tension so productive conversation becomes possible.

Lower Your Voice: Speak more quietly and slowly than the other person. This unconsciously encourages them to match your tone and creates a calmer atmosphere.

Use Neutral Language: Avoid words that trigger defensiveness like "you always" or "you never." Instead, focus on specific behaviors and their impact using the SBI framework from Chapter 6.

Ask Questions: Shift from making statements to asking genuine questions about the other person's perspective. This moves the conversation from argument to inquiry.

Find Common Ground: Identify shared values, goals, or concerns that both parties care about. This creates a foundation for collaborative problem-solving.

Take Breaks: When emotions are too high for productive discussion, suggest taking time to cool down before continuing the conversation.

De-escalation in Action: Marcus's Restaurant Crisis

Marcus faced the ultimate test when an angry customer's complaint about slow service escalated into a public confrontation during peak dinner hours. With other diners watching and his team stressed, Marcus applied the CALM method under pressure.

He began with **Centering** himself—taking a deep breath and lowering his voice deliberately. "I can see you're frustrated, and I want to make this right," he said calmly. **Acknowledging** the customer's experience without defensiveness: "Your meal did take longer than acceptable, and that's on us."

Listening actively, Marcus discovered the real issue—the customer was celebrating an anniversary and felt the experience was ruined. This shifted the conversation from service speed to relationship repair. **Managing** the solution, Marcus offered not just a comped meal but arranged for the kitchen to prepare a special dessert presentation.

The result? The couple stayed, other diners witnessed professional conflict resolution, and Marcus's team learned de-escalation techniques they still use today.

Managing Difficult Personalities

Some conflict stems not from situational disagreements but from challenging personality patterns. While you can't change people's fundamental behavior, you can adapt your approach to work more effectively with different personality types.

The Aggressive Challenger:

- **Approach:** Stay calm and professional, don't take personal attacks personally
- **Strategy:** Acknowledge their passion while redirecting to solutions
- **Script:** "I can see this issue really matters to you. Let's focus on what we can control to improve the situation."

The Passive Resistor:

- **Approach:** Create safe opportunities for honest communication
- **Strategy:** Ask direct questions and give time for responses
- **Script:** "I notice you seem hesitant about this direction. What concerns do you have that we should address?"

The Perfectionist:

- **Approach:** Acknowledge their high standards while managing scope
- **Strategy:** Set clear expectations and deadlines upfront
- **Script:** "I appreciate your attention to detail. Given our timeline, what are the must-have elements versus nice-to-have improvements?"

The Drama Creator:

- **Approach:** Respond to facts, not emotions; redirect to solutions
- **Strategy:** Set boundaries around emotional displays and focus on outcomes
- **Script:** "I understand you're upset. Let's identify the specific issue and work on resolving it."

Building Conflict-Resilient Teams

The best conflict management is prevention through creating team cultures that handle disagreement constructively.

Establishing Conflict Norms: Work with your team to establish explicit agreements about how you'll handle disagreements:

- **Assumption of Positive Intent:** Team members commit to assuming colleagues have good intentions, even when disagreeing
- **Direct Communication:** Issues are addressed directly with involved parties rather than through gossip or triangulation
- **Solution Focus:** Discussions emphasize finding resolutions rather than

assigning blame

· **Respect Boundaries:** Personal attacks, interrupting, and dismissive language are unacceptable

Regular Conflict Check-ins: Include brief conflict assessments in team meetings:

· "Are there any tensions or disagreements we need to address?"
· "What's working well in how we handle different perspectives?"
· "Where do we need to improve our conflict resolution?"

Conflict Recovery Practices: When conflicts do occur, help teams learn from them:

· **After-action reviews** that focus on process improvement
· **Relationship repair** conversations between involved parties
· **Team debriefs** that strengthen overall conflict resilience

Cultural Considerations in Conflict Resolution

Different cultural backgrounds influence how people approach conflict, express disagreement, and seek resolution. Understanding these differences helps you adapt your approach for diverse teams.

High-Context vs. Low-Context Communication: Some cultures value indirect communication and reading between the lines, while others prefer explicit, direct discussion. Adapt your conflict resolution style to match your team members' communication preferences.

Individual vs. Collective Orientation: In individualistic cultures, people may be comfortable with direct confrontation and personal advocacy. In collective cultures, maintaining group harmony and avoiding public disagreement may be more important.

Power Distance Considerations: Some team members may be uncomfortable challenging authority figures or speaking up in group settings due to cultural background. Create multiple avenues for people to raise concerns.

Time Orientation: Different cultures have varying approaches to time and process. Some prefer quick resolution while others value deliberate consensus-building even if it takes longer.

Real-World Applications

Samantha's Generational Bridge-Building
Samantha managed a creative team at a marketing agency where tension had developed between veteran designers (45-55 years old) and recent graduates (22-26 years old). The veterans felt the newcomers lacked respect for established processes, while the younger designers felt their innovative ideas were dismissed.

The Escalation: During a client presentation planning meeting, tensions exploded when senior designer Robert interrupted junior designer Zoe with "That's not how we do things here" after she suggested an interactive social media component. Zoe responded with "Maybe that's why our engagement rates are dropping," leading to a heated exchange that derailed the entire meeting.

Samantha's CALM Approach:
Centering: Rather than choosing sides, Samantha called a break and took time to plan her response. She recognized this was about more than one disagreement—it represented deeper generational tensions affecting team performance.

Acknowledging: She met separately with each group first. To the veterans: "I understand you're concerned about maintaining quality standards and client relationships." To the newcomers: "I hear that you feel your ideas aren't getting fair consideration."

Listening: Through individual conversations, Samantha discovered the real issues. Veterans felt pressured to learn new technologies without proper training. Newcomers felt isolated and undervalued. Both groups actually shared the same goal—creating outstanding work for clients.

Managing: Samantha implemented a "reverse mentoring" program where veterans taught industry knowledge and client management while newcomers led technology workshops. She also established "innovation hours" where new ideas were explored without judgment.

Results: Within three months, the team won their largest client campaign ever—combining the veterans' strategic expertise with innovative digital approaches. Team satisfaction scores increased 40%, and voluntary turnover dropped to zero.

Key Learning: Samantha discovered that generational conflict often masks deeper needs for respect, growth, and contribution. By creating structures that allowed each group to teach and learn, she transformed competition into collaboration.

Marcus's Restaurant Crisis Management

Marcus managed a popular downtown restaurant where a perfect storm of challenges tested every conflict resolution skill. During the busiest Saturday night of the year, their point-of-sale system crashed, the air conditioning failed, and a large party arrived 30 minutes early for their reservation.

The Crisis: Multiple conflicts erupted simultaneously. Servers couldn't process orders efficiently, customers grew increasingly impatient in the heat, and kitchen staff fell behind without digital order tracking. When a prominent food blogger complained loudly about the delays, other diners joined in, creating a hostile atmosphere that threatened to destroy the restaurant's reputation.

Marcus's Multi-Front Response:

Immediate De-escalation: Marcus personally approached each upset table, acknowledging the problems honestly: "I know this isn't the experience you expected. Here's what we're doing to fix it, and here's how we're going to make it right for you."

Team Communication: He gathered his staff for a 60-second huddle: "This is challenging, but we've handled tough nights before. Focus on what you can control, communicate with each other, and remember we're a team."

Creative Problem-Solving: Without the POS system, Marcus had servers write orders on paper and created a manual tracking system using colored cards for different courses. He opened the emergency generator for partial air conditioning and offered complimentary appetizers to all tables.

Stakeholder Management: For the food blogger, Marcus provided a behind-the-scenes look at their crisis response, turning a potential negative review into a story about resilience and customer service.

Long-term Resolution: The experience led to improved emergency procedures, backup systems, and staff cross-training that prevented similar crises.

Results: Despite the technical failures, the restaurant received numerous positive reviews praising their crisis management. The food blogger's article about "grace under pressure" brought new customers, and staff cohesion actually strengthened through shared challenge. Reservation bookings increased 20% over the following month.

Key Learning: Marcus learned that transparent communication and creative problem-solving during crisis could actually strengthen stakeholder relationships rather than damage them.

Jennifer's School District Diplomacy

Jennifer became assistant superintendent of a mid-sized school district during a contentious budget crisis requiring significant cuts. Multiple stakeholder groups—teachers, parents, school board members, and community leaders—had conflicting priorities and were engaging in increasingly hostile public debates.

The Conflict Web: Teachers threatened strikes over proposed layoffs. Parents demanded maintenance of small class sizes and extracurricular programs. The school board faced pressure to keep taxes low while maintaining educational quality. Community members without children questioned education funding priorities.

Jennifer's Systematic Approach:

Stakeholder Mapping: She identified all parties' core interests beyond their stated positions. Teachers needed job security and respect. Parents wanted quality education for their children. Board members needed fiscally responsible solutions. Community members sought transparency and accountability.

Structured Dialogue: Rather than traditional public hearings that became shouting matches, Jennifer organized facilitated small-group sessions where different stakeholders could share perspectives and brainstorm solutions together.

Data-Driven Transparency: She created clear visualizations showing budget constraints, state funding formulas, and the real impact of different cutting scenarios. This helped move conversations from emotional reactions to informed problem-solving.

Creative Partnerships: Jennifer facilitated discussions that led to innovative solutions—local businesses providing internship programs, retired teachers volunteering for certain programs, and community groups fundraising for specific initiatives.

Communication Strategy: She established regular updates through multiple channels, ensuring all stakeholders received consistent, accurate information about decisions and their rationale.

Results: The district avoided strikes and maintained core educational programs while staying within budget. More importantly, the collaborative process strengthened community support for education. Three years later, voters approved a tax increase for school improvements—the first successful education levy in a decade.

Key Learning: Jennifer discovered that stakeholder conflict often escalates when people feel excluded from decision-making processes. By creating structured opportunities for input and collaboration, she transformed adversarial relationships into partnerships.

Reflection Questions:

- Which conflict resolution approach resonates most with your leadership style?
- How might you adapt these strategies to your industry or organizational culture?
- What systems could you implement to catch conflicts earlier?
- How do you currently handle your own emotional responses during tense situations?

This Week's Challenge

Identify one ongoing tension or minor conflict within your team that you've been avoiding. Apply the CALM method this week:

1. **Center** yourself before the conversation
2. **Acknowledge** all perspectives involved
3. **Listen** for underlying interests and concerns
4. **Manage** toward a collaborative solution

Document what happens and what you learn about both the situation and your own conflict resolution capabilities.

* * *

Next Chapter Preview: In Chapter 11, we'll explore how to think strategically about your team's role within the broader organization and develop systems thinking capabilities that help you anticipate and navigate complex challenges before they become crises.

11

Strategic Thinking and Decision-Making

Moving from tactical execution to strategic thinking marks a significant evolution in your management journey. It's the difference between managing today's work and shaping tomorrow's possibilities, between solving immediate problems and preventing future ones.

This chapter explores how to develop strategic thinking capabilities, make decisions with incomplete information, and balance short-term pressures with long-term vision. You'll learn frameworks for analyzing complex situations, involving your team in strategic planning, and making choices that position your team for sustained success.

Developing Strategic Thinking Capabilities

Strategic thinking is often misunderstood as only relevant for senior executives, but every level of management benefits from the ability to see patterns, anticipate changes, and make decisions that serve both immediate and future needs. For new managers, developing strategic thinking capabilities is essential for career progression and team effectiveness.

What Strategic Thinking Really Means

Strategic thinking isn't just long-term planning—it's a way of approaching problems and opportunities that considers multiple perspectives, anticipates consequences, and connects today's actions to tomorrow's outcomes.

Core Components of Strategic Thinking:

Systems Thinking: Understanding how different parts of the organization, market, or industry connect and influence each other. This means recognizing that changes in one area often create ripple effects elsewhere.

Pattern Recognition: Identifying trends, cycles, and recurring themes that can inform future planning. This involves looking at historical data, market signals, and organizational patterns to spot emerging opportunities or threats.

Future Orientation: Balancing immediate needs with longer-term implications. Strategic thinkers consider how today's decisions will impact capabilities, relationships, and opportunities months or years ahead.

Outside-In Perspective: Looking beyond internal operations to understand customer needs, competitive dynamics, technological changes, and broader market forces that could affect the business.

Resource Optimization: Thinking about how to best allocate limited resources—time, money, people, attention—to achieve maximum impact across multiple priorities.

The Strategic vs. Tactical Mindset Shift

Many new managers struggle with the transition from tactical execution to strategic thinking because it requires a fundamental shift in how they approach their role.

Tactical Mindset:

- Focuses on completing tasks efficiently

- Optimizes current processes and systems
- Reacts to problems as they arise
- Measures success by output and activity
- Works within existing constraints

Strategic Mindset:

- Focuses on identifying opportunities and potential challenges
- Questions existing processes and seeks innovation
- Anticipates problems and creates preventive solutions
- Measures success by long-term outcomes and impact
- Challenges constraints and seeks new possibilities

This shift doesn't mean abandoning tactical excellence—rather, it means developing the ability to operate at both levels simultaneously, ensuring today's work serves tomorrow's goals.

Building Strategic Awareness

Environmental Scanning: Regularly gather information about trends and changes that could affect your team or organization:

Industry Intelligence: Monitor competitors, industry reports, and market research to understand evolving dynamics.

Customer Intelligence: Ongoing collection of customer feedback, needs analysis, and behavior patterns to anticipate changing requirements.

Technology Monitoring: Awareness of technological developments that could impact your work processes, industry, or customer expectations.

Regulatory Awareness: Understanding of policy, legal, and regulatory changes that might affect operations or create new opportunities.

Economic Indicators: Monitoring of broader economic trends that could impact budgets, hiring, or strategic priorities.

SWOT Analysis for Teams: Regularly assess your team's position using

Strengths, Weaknesses, Opportunities, and Threats analysis:

Strengths: What unique capabilities does your team have? What do you do better than others?

Weaknesses: Where are your skill gaps or resource constraints? What limits your effectiveness?

Opportunities: What external changes could benefit your team? What emerging needs could you address?

Threats: What external factors could harm your team's success? What competitive or technological changes pose risks?

Strategic Planning at the Team Level

Strategic thinking becomes actionable through planning processes that connect vision to execution while maintaining flexibility for changing circumstances.

The Team Strategic Planning Process:

1. Vision Clarification (Building on Chapter 4):

- Revisit and refine your team's purpose and long-term aspirations
- Ensure alignment with organizational strategy
- Consider how external changes might affect your vision

2. Situation Analysis:

- Conduct thorough environmental scanning
- Assess current capabilities and performance
- Identify key success factors and constraints

3. Strategic Options Generation:

- Brainstorm multiple potential approaches to achieving your vision
- Consider different scenarios and contingencies

- Evaluate trade-offs and resource requirements

4. Priority Setting:

- Choose strategic focus areas based on impact and feasibility
- Allocate resources according to strategic priorities
- Establish clear success metrics and timelines

5. Implementation Planning:

- Break strategic goals into operational objectives
- Assign responsibilities and create accountability systems
- Build in regular review and adjustment mechanisms

Developing Team Strategic Thinking

Strategic thinking shouldn't be limited to the manager—involving your entire team in strategic discussions strengthens decision-making and builds organizational capability.

Team Strategic Thinking Activities:
Scenario Planning Sessions: Work together to imagine different possible futures and how your team would respond to each scenario.
Competitive Analysis: Have team members research and present findings about competitors, best practices, or industry trends.
Customer Journey Mapping: Collaboratively analyze how customers experience your products or services and identify improvement opportunities.
Innovation Labs: Dedicate time for team members to explore new ideas, technologies, or approaches that could benefit your work.
Strategic Book Club: Read and discuss books about strategy, industry trends, or business thinking as a team.

Decision-Making Frameworks and Tools

Effective decision-making is where strategic thinking meets practical action. New managers need frameworks that help them make good decisions quickly while involving their team appropriately and learning from outcomes.

Understanding Decision Types and Approaches

Not all decisions require the same level of analysis or involvement. Understanding different decision types helps managers choose appropriate approaches and avoid both over-analysis and under-consideration.

Decision Classification Framework:
Type 1 Decisions (Reversible):

- Consequences are not permanent
- Can be changed or reversed if they don't work
- Should be made quickly with available information
- Example: Trial period for a new software tool

Type 2 Decisions (Irreversible):

- Have long-lasting or permanent consequences
- Difficult or impossible to reverse
- Warrant thorough analysis and stakeholder input
- Example: Hiring decisions or major strategic shifts

Frequency-Based Classification:

- **Routine Decisions:** Regular, operational choices that can be systematized or delegated
- **Adaptive Decisions:** Require adjustment of existing approaches to new circumstances

- **Innovative Decisions:** Create new approaches to unprecedented situations

The DECIDE Framework

For complex decisions that require structured analysis, the DECIDE framework provides a comprehensive approach:

D - Define the Problem Clearly:

- What exactly needs to be decided?
- Why is this decision necessary now?
- What are the constraints and requirements?
- Who are the stakeholders affected by this decision?

E - Evaluate Alternatives:

- Generate multiple potential options
- Consider both obvious and creative alternatives
- Include the option of not making a change
- Research precedents and best practices

C - Consider Consequences:

- Analyze potential outcomes of each alternative
- Consider both intended and unintended consequences
- Evaluate short-term and long-term implications
- Assess risks and mitigation strategies

I - Identify Values and Preferences:

- Clarify decision criteria and priorities
- Consider organizational values and culture

- Weigh stakeholder preferences and concerns
- Determine success metrics

D – Decide and Document:

- Choose the best alternative based on analysis
- Document reasoning and decision criteria
- Communicate decision and rationale clearly
- Establish accountability and next steps

E – Evaluate the Decision:

- Monitor outcomes and gather feedback
- Assess whether objectives are being met
- Learn from both successes and failures
- Adjust approach if necessary

Decision-Making in Uncertainty

Many management decisions must be made with incomplete information and uncertain outcomes. This requires comfort with ambiguity and frameworks for making good choices despite uncertainty.

Strategies for Uncertain Decisions:

Probabilistic Thinking: Instead of seeking certainty, estimate probabilities and make decisions based on expected values and risk tolerance.

Reversibility Assessment: Prioritize decisions that can be adjusted or reversed if new information emerges, allowing for experimentation and learning.

Minimum Viable Decisions: Make the smallest decision possible that moves you forward, then gather more information before committing to larger choices.

Scenario Planning: Consider multiple possible futures and choose strategies that perform reasonably well across different scenarios.

Real Options Thinking: Structure decisions to preserve future choices and flexibility rather than committing to single paths.

Involving Others in Decision-Making

Knowing when and how to involve your team in decisions is crucial for both decision quality and team development. The communication and inclusion skills from previous chapters become essential here.

The Participation Spectrum:

Inform: You make the decision and communicate it to the team

- Use when: Decision is routine, time-sensitive, or within your clear authority
- Benefits: Speed and efficiency
- Risks: Lack of buy-in or missing important information

Consult: You gather input from others but make the final decision

- Use when: You need expertise or perspectives you don't have
- Benefits: Better information and some stakeholder buy-in
- Risks: People may feel consulted but not heard

Collaborate: You work with others to make the decision together

- Use when: Decision affects multiple people and you need strong commitment
- Benefits: High buy-in and diverse perspectives
- Risks: Slower process and potential for compromise solutions

Delegate: You give decision-making authority to others

- Use when: Others have better information or when development is a priority
- Benefits: Empowerment and development opportunities
- Risks: Decisions may not align with your preferences

Cognitive Biases in Decision-Making

Understanding common decision-making biases helps managers make more objective choices and design processes that counteract natural mental shortcuts.

Common Decision Biases:

Confirmation Bias: Seeking information that confirms existing beliefs while ignoring contradictory evidence.

- Mitigation: Actively seek disconfirming evidence and devil's advocate perspectives

Anchoring Bias: Over-relying on the first piece of information encountered.

- Mitigation: Consider multiple reference points and question initial assumptions

Availability Bias: Overweighting recent or memorable events when assessing probabilities.

- Mitigation: Use data and systematic analysis rather than relying on memory

Sunk Cost Fallacy: Continuing investments based on past costs rather than future benefits.

- Mitigation: Focus on future value and ignore non-recoverable past investments

Groupthink: Pressure for harmony leading to poor decisions and lack of critical evaluation.

· Mitigation: Encourage dissent, use structured decision processes, and bring in outside perspectives

Data-Driven Decision Making

While intuition and experience remain important, incorporating data analysis into decision-making improves accuracy and reduces bias.

Building Data-Driven Practices

Identify Key Metrics: Determine what data is most relevant for the types of decisions you make regularly.

Create Measurement Systems: Establish processes for collecting, analyzing, and reporting relevant data consistently.

Develop Analytics Skills: Build capability in your team to interpret data and extract actionable insights.

Balance Data with Judgment: Use data to inform decisions while recognizing its limitations and the continued importance of experience and intuition.

Test and Learn Approaches: Design experiments and pilot programs that generate data about what works before making large-scale commitments.

Case Study Integration: Sarah's Digital Transformation Decision

Sarah, a 39-year-old operations manager at a mid-sized logistics company, faced a complex decision about whether to implement AI-powered routing software that promised 25% efficiency gains but required substantial investment and change management.

The Decision Challenge: The software vendor claimed significant benefits, but implementation would require retraining 40 staff members, integrating with legacy systems, and changing established workflows. The decision had to be made within six weeks to secure early-adopter pricing.

DECIDE Framework Application:

Define: Sarah clearly articulated the decision: whether to implement AI routing software within the early-adopter window, considering costs, benefits, risks, and organizational readiness.

Evaluate Alternatives:

- Implement the AI software immediately
- Delay implementation for better preparation
- Pilot the software with a small team first
- Continue with current systems and evaluate other vendors

Consider Consequences: Sarah analyzed potential outcomes:

- Immediate implementation: High efficiency gains but significant disruption risk
- Delay: Miss cost savings but allow better preparation
- Pilot: Reduced risk but delayed benefits and potential increased costs
- Status quo: No disruption but competitive disadvantage

Identify Values: The company prioritized customer service, employee development, and sustainable growth over short-term cost savings.

Decide: Sarah chose the pilot approach, negotiating with the vendor to test the software with two major clients while maintaining current systems for others.

Evaluate: The pilot revealed integration challenges the vendor hadn't mentioned but confirmed efficiency benefits. Sarah used this data to negotiate better terms and implementation support for full rollout.

Results:

- The pilot prevented costly system failures that would have occurred with immediate full implementation
- Efficiency gains of 18% (slightly below vendor promises but still substantial)
- Zero employee turnover during transition due to gradual change management
- The company became a case study for successful AI implementation in logistics

Key Learning: Sarah discovered that structured decision-making frameworks are most valuable for complex, high-stakes decisions where emotions and time pressure can lead to poor choices. The DECIDE process forced her to consider alternatives she hadn't initially evaluated and make a more informed choice.

Developing strategic thinking and decision-making capabilities is a gradual process that improves with practice and reflection. The frameworks and tools in this chapter provide structure for approaching complex choices, but they must be adapted to your specific context and circumstances.

The strategic thinking skills you develop will serve you throughout your career, enabling you to navigate uncertainty, anticipate challenges, and position your team for long-term success.

This Week's Challenge

Apply strategic thinking to a current challenge:

1. **Identify one significant decision** your team will need to make in the next month
2. **Conduct a mini-SWOT analysis** of your team's current position
3. **Use the DECIDE framework** to structure your approach to the upcoming decision
4. **Involve your team** in strategic thinking through one of the activities

mentioned (scenario planning, competitive analysis, etc.)

5. **Set up systems** for ongoing environmental scanning in your area

* * *

Next Chapter Preview: In Chapter 12, we'll explore how to lead through crisis and build resilience, building on the strategic thinking and decision-making skills you've developed to navigate unexpected challenges, maintain team effectiveness under pressure, and emerge stronger from difficult situations.

12

Crisis Management and Resilience

Crisis will find you whether you're prepared or not. The question isn't if you'll face unexpected challenges, but how effectively you'll respond when they arrive. Some managers freeze, hoping problems will resolve themselves. Others react impulsively, creating additional chaos. The most effective leaders develop systematic approaches that help them navigate turbulence while maintaining team cohesion and organizational effectiveness.

Crisis management isn't about having perfect answers—it's about having reliable processes that help you make good decisions under pressure, communicate clearly when information is limited, and support your team through uncertainty. This chapter provides frameworks for different types of crises and strategies for building both personal and team resilience.

Understanding Crisis Types and Characteristics

Not all crises are created equal. Understanding different crisis categories helps you choose appropriate response strategies and allocate resources effectively.

Operational Crises affect day-to-day business functions—system failures, supply chain disruptions, or key personnel departures. These typically have clear causes and solutions but require rapid coordination.

Strategic Crises threaten long-term organizational viability—market shifts, competitive threats, or regulatory changes. These require thoughtful analysis and often fundamental operational adjustments.

Reputational Crises damage public trust and stakeholder confidence—ethical violations, public relations disasters, or social media controversies. These demand careful communication and relationship repair.

External Crises originate outside your organization—natural disasters, economic downturns, or industry-wide disruptions. These require adaptation to circumstances beyond your control.

Most real crises combine elements from multiple categories. The COVID-19 pandemic, for example, created operational challenges (remote work), strategic pressures (business model adaptation), reputational concerns (health and safety), and external disruption (economic uncertainty) simultaneously.

Crisis Characteristics That Affect Response

Speed and Pressure: Some crises demand immediate action while others allow time for deliberate planning. Understanding which type you're facing prevents both premature decisions and dangerous delays.

Information Availability: Crisis decisions often must be made with incomplete information. Building comfort with uncertainty and creating processes for gathering information quickly becomes essential.

Stakeholder Impact: Consider who is affected and how—employees, customers, partners, regulators, and community members may all require different types of communication and support.

Resource Requirements: Assess what you'll need—additional staff, financial resources, expertise, or technology—and how quickly you can access these resources.

The Psychology of Crisis Response

Understanding how people respond to crisis helps you lead more effectively during challenging times. Crisis triggers predictable psychological patterns that affect decision-making and team dynamics.

Fight, Flight, or Freeze: Under stress, people default to one of these responses. Some become hyperactive and take on too much. Others avoid decision-making or withdraw from responsibilities. Still others become paralyzed by uncertainty. Recognizing these patterns in yourself and your team helps you provide appropriate support.

Cognitive Overload: Crisis creates information overwhelm that impairs judgment. People struggle to process multiple variables simultaneously and may focus on the wrong priorities. Providing structure and breaking problems into manageable pieces helps maintain clear thinking.

Emotional Volatility: Stress amplifies emotions—both positive and negative. Team members may become more irritable, anxious, or overwhelmed than usual. Some may also discover reserves of creativity and determination they didn't know they possessed.

Communication Breakdown: Under pressure, people often communicate less effectively—making assumptions, avoiding difficult conversations, or becoming overly blunt. Establishing clear communication protocols becomes critical.

Building Personal Crisis Resilience

Your effectiveness during crisis depends on your ability to manage your own stress and maintain clear thinking under pressure.

Stress Management Techniques:

- **Breathing and Grounding:** Use controlled breathing to maintain calm. The 4-7-8 technique (inhale for 4, hold for 7, exhale for 8) helps reset your nervous system.
- **Physical Movement:** Even brief walks or stretching can help process stress and maintain energy.
- **Cognitive Reframing:** Focus on what you can control rather than dwelling on circumstances beyond your influence.
- **Information Hygiene:** Limit exposure to excessive negative information that doesn't help your decision-making.

Decision-Making Under Pressure: Frank's experience during the COVID crisis demonstrates these principles in action. As the emergency department director at a 400-bed hospital, he faced unprecedented challenges when the pandemic hit his community.

The RAPID Framework for Crisis Decision-Making

When facing crisis decisions with limited time and information, the RAPID framework provides structure for making good choices under pressure:

R - Recognize the Situation Quickly assess what you're dealing with and what decisions need to be made immediately versus what can wait.

A - Assemble Information Gather the most critical information available, but don't wait for perfect data. Set time limits for information gathering.

P - Process Options Generate multiple alternatives quickly. Include both obvious solutions and creative alternatives.

I - Implement with Clear Communication Choose your course of action and communicate it clearly to all stakeholders with rationale and next steps.

D - Debrief and Adjust Monitor results and adjust your approach as new information becomes available.

Frank applied this framework throughout the early weeks of the pandemic. When the hospital's PPE supplies ran critically low, he **Recognized** this as an immediate operational crisis requiring rapid action. He **Assembled** information about supply chain options, usage rates, and regulatory alternatives. He **Processed** options including emergency procurement, usage protocol changes, and community partnerships. He **Implemented** a multi-pronged approach including rationing protocols and local manufacturer partnerships. Finally, he **Debriefed** daily with his team to adjust based on changing conditions.

Crisis Communication Strategies

Effective communication during crisis builds trust, reduces anxiety, and coordinates effective response. Poor communication amplifies problems and creates additional conflicts.

Transparency with Boundaries: Share what you know while acknowledging what you don't know. Avoid speculation or false reassurance, but don't overwhelm people with every uncertainty.

Regular Updates: Establish predictable communication rhythms so stakeholders know when to expect information. Even if you have no new information, confirm that you're monitoring the situation.

Multi-Channel Approach: Use various communication methods to ensure important information reaches everyone—email, meetings, informal check-ins, and visual displays.

Stakeholder-Specific Messaging: Different groups need different levels of detail and different types of reassurance. Your team needs tactical information while your boss may need strategic implications.

Supporting Your Team Through Crisis

Your team's effectiveness during crisis depends on both practical support and emotional leadership.

Practical Support Strategies:

- **Clear Priorities:** Help team members understand what's most important when everything feels urgent
- **Resource Access:** Ensure people have the tools, information, and authority they need to do their jobs
- **Workload Management:** Monitor stress levels and redistribute work when necessary
- **Skill Development:** Provide quick training on new procedures or technologies required by changing circumstances

Emotional Leadership:

- **Presence:** Be visible and available without micromanaging
- **Calm Confidence:** Model the emotional tone you want from your team
- **Recognition:** Acknowledge extra efforts and small wins during difficult times
- **Individual Check-ins:** Understand how crisis is affecting different team members personally

Frank's approach to team support proved crucial during the most intense period of the pandemic response. He established daily team huddles that lasted exactly 15 minutes and followed a consistent format: situation update, resource status, individual concerns, and one positive recognition. This predictability became an anchor during chaotic days.

For team members struggling with different aspects of the crisis, Frank adapted his approach. For anxious staff, he provided detailed safety protocols and regular health updates. For overwhelmed team members, he helped prioritize and delegate. For those who thrived under pressure, he channeled their energy into training and process improvement projects.

Post-Crisis Learning and Recovery

How you handle the aftermath of crisis determines whether your organization emerges stronger or simply returns to previous vulnerabilities.

Systematic After-Action Review: Conduct thorough analysis while events are still fresh in everyone's memory:

- **What Worked Well:** Identify successful strategies and decisions that should be maintained or expanded
- **What Could Be Improved:** Analyze decisions and processes that weren't optimal without assigning blame
- **What We Learned:** Capture insights about your organization, team, and external environment
- **How We'll Prepare Better:** Develop specific action items for improved future readiness

Organizational Changes: Crisis often reveals weaknesses in systems, processes, or culture that weren't apparent during normal operations. Use these insights to make meaningful improvements:

- **Process Improvements:** Update procedures based on what you learned about bottlenecks and inefficiencies
- **Capability Building:** Invest in training and resources that would have helped during the crisis
- **Relationship Strengthening:** Deepen partnerships and communication channels that proved valuable

- **Cultural Evolution:** Reinforce values and behaviors that served you well while addressing patterns that didn't

Individual Recovery: Help team members process their crisis experience and integrate lessons learned:

- **Recognition:** Acknowledge the extra effort and sacrifice people made during difficult times
- **Reflection:** Provide opportunities for people to share their experiences and insights
- **Development:** Identify skills and capabilities individuals developed that can be leveraged going forward
- **Rest and Renewal:** Ensure people have time to recover before tackling the next major challenge

Building Organizational Resilience

The most effective crisis management is prevention through building organizational resilience—the ability to anticipate, adapt to, and recover from challenges.

Systems Thinking: Understand how different parts of your organization connect and how problems in one area can cascade to others. Regular "what if" discussions help identify vulnerabilities.

Scenario Planning: Work with your team to imagine possible future challenges and discuss how you might respond. This builds both practical preparedness and psychological readiness.

Redundancy and Flexibility: Build backup systems and alternative approaches for critical functions. Cross-train team members so operations can continue despite individual absences.

Relationship Investment: Strong relationships with colleagues, customers, partners, and stakeholders provide crucial support during difficult times. Invest in these connections before you need them.

Learning Culture: Organizations that encourage experimentation, tolerate failure, and capture lessons are better equipped to adapt when circumstances change.

Real-World Application

Frank's COVID-19 Hospital Crisis Leadership

Frank became the emergency department director at Metropolitan General Hospital just six months before COVID-19 reached his community. With limited management experience but strong clinical skills, he suddenly found himself leading 47 staff members through the most challenging period in modern healthcare.

The Gathering Storm (Week 1): When the first COVID cases appeared, Frank faced immediate operational crises. PPE supplies were insufficient, testing protocols kept changing, and staff anxiety was escalating. Using the RAPID framework, Frank **Recognized** that this was unlike any crisis the hospital had faced—requiring both immediate tactical responses and longer-term strategic adaptation.

Information Gathering and Decision Making: Frank **Assembled** information from multiple sources—CDC guidelines, state health department directives, supply chain partners, and other hospital directors. He discovered that traditional approaches weren't adequate for this unprecedented situation.

Processing Creative Solutions: Rather than waiting for perfect information, Frank **Processed** options that combined standard protocols with innovative approaches. He partnered with local manufacturers to produce face shields, implemented telemedicine protocols to reduce exposure, and created exposure risk assessments for all staff positions.

Implementation Under Pressure: Frank **Implemented** changes rapidly while maintaining clear communication. He established twice-daily all-staff updates, created visual dashboards showing PPE levels and patient status, and developed new protocols for patient flow and staff protection.

The Peak Crisis (Weeks 3-8): During the surge, Frank's department treated over 2,800 suspected COVID patients while maintaining normal emergency services. Staff worked extended shifts, faced personal health fears, and dealt with unprecedented patient volumes.

Frank's leadership during this period demonstrated advanced crisis management:

Adaptive Resource Management: When ICU capacity reached limits, Frank worked with other departments to create overflow protocols. He cross-trained staff for multiple roles and implemented innovative patient tracking systems.

Emotional Leadership: Recognizing that technical skills alone weren't sufficient, Frank focused heavily on team morale. He arranged for meal deliveries during long shifts, created childcare solutions for staff families, and personally checked in with every team member weekly.

Stakeholder Communication: Frank managed complex communication with hospital administration, public health officials, patient families, and media—each requiring different information and reassurance levels.

Continuous Learning: Throughout the crisis, Frank held brief after-action reviews at the end of each shift, capturing what worked and what needed adjustment. This continuous improvement approach helped the team adapt quickly to changing conditions.

Recovery and Growth (Weeks 9-12): As case numbers stabilized, Frank led systematic recovery efforts. The department had achieved remarkable results—they maintained a 15% lower mortality rate than regional averages, lost zero staff to resignations, and received state recognition as a model COVID response unit.

Post-Crisis Analysis: Frank's comprehensive after-action review revealed several key insights:

- **Relationship strength** proved more important than technical resources. Strong teamwork and trust enabled innovative solutions that overcame resource limitations.
- **Communication rhythm** was crucial. Predictable updates reduced anxiety even when information was uncertain.
- **Individual adaptation** varied significantly. Staff needed different types of support based on their personal circumstances and stress responses.
- **Systems thinking** helped anticipate problems. Understanding how different hospital departments connected prevented cascading failures.

Long-term Impact: Frank's crisis leadership led to his promotion to director of emergency services and implementation of his crisis management protocols across the hospital system. Team cohesion scores increased 40% post-crisis, and the department achieved the lowest voluntary turnover rate in hospital history.

Lessons for All Managers: Frank's experience demonstrates that effective crisis leadership combines systematic approaches with adaptive thinking and emotional intelligence. His success came not from having perfect answers but from creating processes that helped his team navigate uncertainty together while maintaining focus on their core mission of patient care.

Reflection Questions:

- How would you adapt Frank's RAPID framework to crises in your industry?
- What relationships and resources would be most critical during a crisis in your organization?
- How might you build crisis resilience into your team's normal operations?
- What aspects of your current stress management need strengthening before the next crisis?

This Week's Challenge

Conduct a crisis preparedness assessment with your team:

1. **Identify potential crisis scenarios** that could affect your department
2. **Map your current resources** and response capabilities
3. **Develop basic response protocols** for the most likely scenarios
4. **Establish communication plans** for different stakeholder groups
5. **Schedule regular check-ins** to update and practice these plans

Remember: the goal isn't to predict every possible crisis but to build the capabilities and relationships that help you respond effectively to unexpected challenges.

* * *

Next Chapter Preview: In Chapter 13, we'll explore how to lead organizational change and transformation, building on the crisis management skills you've developed to guide your team through planned transitions and strategic shifts.

IV

Part IV: Growing as a Future-Ready Leader

Future-focused growth

Prepare for the evolving demands of leadership while building sustainable habits for long-term growth, impact, and career success in an ever-changing workplace.

13

The Future of Leadership

Leadership is evolving rapidly in response to technological advances, changing workforce expectations, and global challenges that require new approaches to creating value and managing people. Understanding these trends helps you develop capabilities that will remain relevant as the leadership landscape continues to shift.

This chapter explores emerging leadership competencies, the role of technology in management, and how to prepare yourself and your team for an uncertain but opportunity-rich future. You'll discover how to stay adaptable while maintaining the human-centered leadership skills that will always matter.

The Changing Leadership Landscape

The leadership challenges of today differ significantly from those of even a decade ago. Remote work, artificial intelligence, climate concerns, social justice awareness, and rapid technological change have created new expectations for what effective leadership looks like.

Key Trends Reshaping Leadership

Distributed Authority: Organizations are becoming flatter and more networked, requiring leaders who can influence without formal authority and collaborate across boundaries.

Purpose-Driven Work: Employees increasingly seek meaning and impact in their work, requiring leaders who can connect daily tasks to larger purposes and values.

Continuous Learning: The pace of change demands leaders who can learn rapidly and help their teams develop new capabilities continuously.

Stakeholder Complexity: Leaders must balance the needs of diverse stakeholders—employees, customers, communities, environment, and shareholders—rather than focusing solely on financial performance.

Digital-Physical Integration: Hybrid work and digital transformation require leaders who can manage both virtual and in-person relationships effectively.

The Evolving Definition of Leadership Success

Traditional leadership success metrics—financial performance, efficiency, and growth—remain important but are no longer sufficient. Future leaders will be evaluated on broader criteria:

Sustainable Performance: Achieving results in ways that can be maintained over time without depleting human or environmental resources.

Inclusive Excellence: Creating high performance while ensuring all team members can contribute their best work regardless of background or identity.

Adaptive Capacity: Building organizations and teams that can respond effectively to unexpected challenges and opportunities.

Social Impact: Contributing positively to community and societal well-being beyond immediate business objectives.

Learning Velocity: Developing personal and organizational capabilities faster than the pace of external change.

Emerging Leadership Competencies

Future-ready leaders will need to develop new capabilities while maintaining the foundational skills that have always been essential for effective leadership.

Digital Leadership Skills

Technology Fluency: Understanding how technology affects your industry and team's work, even if you're not a technical expert yourself.

Data Literacy: Ability to interpret and use data for decision-making while recognizing its limitations and potential biases.

Virtual Relationship Building: Creating trust and connection through digital channels, managing remote teams, and facilitating online collaboration.

Digital Communication: Mastering various digital communication tools and knowing when to use each for maximum effectiveness.

Cybersecurity Awareness: Understanding security risks and best practices to protect both your organization and team members.

Emotional and Social Intelligence Evolution

Cultural Competence: Working effectively with people from diverse cultural backgrounds, understanding different communication styles and values.

Generational Bridge-Building: Managing teams that span multiple generations with different work styles, values, and expectations.

Empathy at Scale: Demonstrating care and understanding for large groups of people, not just immediate team members.

Difficult Conversation Navigation: Addressing sensitive topics like bias, inequality, mental health, and social justice with skill and authenticity.

Burnout Prevention: Recognizing signs of stress and overwhelm in yourself and others, creating sustainable work practices.

Strategic and Systems Thinking

Complexity Navigation: Handling situations with multiple stakeholders, conflicting priorities, and uncertain outcomes.

Future Scenario Planning: Thinking through multiple possible futures and preparing for different contingencies.

Sustainability Mindset: Considering environmental and social impact in business decisions, balancing profit with purpose.

Network Leadership: Influencing and coordinating across organizational boundaries, building coalitions and partnerships.

Innovation Facilitation: Creating conditions where new ideas can emerge, experiment safely, and scale effectively.

Technology's Role in Future Management

Technology will continue to transform how managers work, requiring adaptation while maintaining focus on fundamentally human aspects of leadership.

AI and Automation Impact

Decision Support: AI tools will provide data analysis and pattern recognition to inform management decisions while requiring human judgment for interpretation and implementation.

Administrative Automation: Routine management tasks like scheduling, reporting, and performance tracking will become increasingly automated, freeing managers to focus on strategy and relationship building.

Personalized Development: Technology will enable more customized learning and development plans for team members based on their individual needs and goals.

Predictive Analytics: Managers will have access to tools that can predict team performance issues, turnover risks, and project outcomes with increasing accuracy.

Human-AI Collaboration

Augmented Leadership: The most effective future managers will combine human emotional intelligence with AI analytical capabilities rather than viewing them as competing approaches.

Ethical AI Use: Leaders will need to ensure AI tools are used responsibly, addressing bias in algorithms and maintaining human oversight of important decisions.

Change Management: Helping teams adapt to AI and automation while managing concerns about job displacement and changing skill requirements.

Value Creation Focus: As routine tasks become automated, managers will increasingly focus on activities that create unique human value—creativity, empathy, complex problem-solving, and relationship building.

Digital Transformation Leadership

Change Facilitation: Leading technological transitions while maintaining team cohesion and performance.

Learning Culture Development: Creating environments where continuous learning and adaptation become natural parts of team culture.

Technology Integration: Understanding how new tools can enhance rather than replace human capabilities.

Digital Divide Management: Ensuring all team members can access and effectively use required technologies.

Building Future-Ready Teams

Preparing your team for an uncertain future requires developing capabilities that will remain valuable regardless of specific technological or market changes.

Core Future-Ready Capabilities

Learning Agility: The ability to quickly acquire new skills and knowledge as circumstances change.

Adaptability: Comfort with ambiguity and change, resilience in the face of setbacks.

Critical Thinking: Ability to analyze information objectively and make reasoned judgments.

Creative Problem-Solving: Generating innovative solutions to novel challenges.

Collaboration Skills: Working effectively with diverse people across different contexts and communication channels.

Emotional Resilience: Managing stress and maintaining effectiveness during difficult periods.

Future-Ready Development Strategies

Cross-Functional Learning: Encourage team members to understand how different parts of the organization work together.

External Perspective Building: Provide opportunities for team members to interact with customers, partners, and industry peers.

Experimentation Culture: Create safe spaces for trying new approaches and learning from failures.

Continuous Feedback: Implement regular feedback systems that help people adjust and improve continuously.

Network Building: Help team members develop professional relationships that extend beyond your immediate organization.

Case Study Integration: Alex's Manufacturing Innovation

Alex, a 45-year-old plant manager at a traditional manufacturing company, faced the challenge of implementing Industry 4.0 technologies while maintaining productivity and managing workforce concerns about automation.

The Future-Ready Challenge: The company needed to implement IoT sensors, predictive maintenance algorithms, and automated quality control systems to remain competitive, but many workers feared job displacement.

Building Future-Ready Capabilities:

Learning Culture Development: Alex established "Innovation Fridays" where workers could experiment with new technologies and suggest improvements to existing processes.

Cross-Training Programs: He implemented systematic cross-training so workers could operate multiple types of equipment and understand broader production systems.

Technology Partnership: Alex paired experienced workers with engineers implementing new systems, creating mutual learning opportunities.

Change Communication: He held regular town halls explaining how technology would augment rather than replace human capabilities, with specific examples of how jobs would evolve.

Skills Development: The company partnered with a local community college to provide certificate programs in digital manufacturing and data analysis.

Innovation Recognition: Alex created awards for employees who suggested improvements or successfully adapted to new technologies.

Results:

- Successful implementation of smart manufacturing systems with zero involuntary layoffs
- 30% improvement in production efficiency and 25% reduction in defects
- 15 employees completed additional technical certifications
- Worker satisfaction scores increased during the transition period
- The plant became a showcase for successful digital transformation

Key Learning: Alex discovered that future-readiness isn't just about technology—it's about creating cultures where people feel excited about change rather than threatened by it. Success came from treating workers as partners in innovation rather than obstacles to overcome.

Preparing for Uncertainty

The pace of change means that specific predictions about the future are less valuable than developing general adaptability and resilience.

Building Adaptive Capacity

Scenario Thinking: Regularly consider multiple possible futures and how your team would respond to different challenges and opportunities.

Diverse Perspectives: Seek input from people with different backgrounds, experiences, and viewpoints to avoid blind spots.

Experimentation Mindset: Treat new approaches as experiments to learn from rather than permanent commitments that must succeed.

Network Development: Build relationships across industries and functions to stay informed about emerging trends and opportunities.

Continuous Learning: Maintain curiosity and invest in ongoing development for yourself and your team.

Maintaining Core Human Values

While leadership methods will continue evolving, certain human values and needs will remain constant:

Trust and Authenticity: People will always need leaders they can trust and who demonstrate genuine care for their well-being.

Meaning and Purpose: The human need to feel that work matters and contributes to something meaningful will persist.

Growth and Development: People will continue to want opportunities to learn, develop, and achieve their potential.

Connection and Belonging: The need for positive relationships and sense of community remains fundamental to human motivation.

Recognition and Appreciation: Acknowledgment of contributions and accomplishments will always be important for engagement and satisfaction.

The future of leadership will be defined by the ability to navigate complexity, leverage technology while maintaining human connection, and create value for diverse stakeholders in rapidly changing environments. The leaders who thrive will be those who develop future-ready capabilities while maintaining the foundational leadership skills that have always mattered—building trust, communicating effectively, and helping people achieve their potential.

Your investment in developing these emerging leadership capabilities, combined with the solid foundation you've built through the previous chapters, positions you to succeed regardless of how the leadership landscape continues to evolve.

This Week's Challenge

Begin preparing for future leadership demands:

1. **Assess your current technology fluency** and identify one area for development
2. **Experiment with one new digital tool** that could improve your team's effectiveness
3. **Conduct a team discussion** about future trends affecting your industry
4. **Identify one future-ready capability** to develop in your team over the next quarter
5. **Build one new relationship** outside your immediate organization to expand your perspective

* * *

Next Chapter Preview: In Chapter 14, we'll explore how to sustain your growth and impact as a leader over the long term, building habits and systems that support continued development and effectiveness.

14

Sustaining Growth, Confidence, and Impact as a Manager

The transition into management is just the beginning of a lifelong journey of growth and development. Sustaining effectiveness over time requires building habits, systems, and perspectives that support continuous improvement while maintaining energy and enthusiasm for the work.

This chapter focuses on creating sustainable practices for ongoing development, building confidence that grows with experience, and maximizing your positive impact as a leader. You'll discover how to avoid common pitfalls that derail promising managers and establish patterns that support long-term success and satisfaction.

Building Sustainable Leadership Habits

The difference between managers who burn out or plateau and those who continue growing and thriving often comes down to the daily habits and systems they establish. Sustainable leadership requires practices that can be maintained over years and decades, not just during the initial enthusiasm of a new role.

The Power of Leadership Habits

Leadership effectiveness isn't primarily about grand gestures or major decisions—it's about the accumulation of small, consistent actions that build trust, develop others, and create positive change over time. Building the right habits creates reliable patterns that serve you well even during stressful or chaotic periods.

Core Leadership Habits for Sustainability:

Daily Connection: Establish regular practices for connecting with team members, even briefly. This might be morning check-ins, informal conversations, or end-of-day progress shares that keep you connected to your team's experience.

Continuous Learning: Dedicate consistent time to learning—reading articles, listening to podcasts, attending webinars, or participating in professional development. Small, regular investments compound over time.

Reflection Practice: Build regular time for reflection into your schedule. This might be weekly reviews of what went well and what to improve, monthly goal assessment, or quarterly strategic thinking sessions.

Self-Care Maintenance: Develop sustainable practices for managing your own energy, stress, and well-being. Leadership requires sustained energy, which demands attention to physical health, mental clarity, and emotional resilience.

Network Cultivation: Consistently invest in relationships with peers, mentors, and industry connections. These relationships provide support, perspective, and opportunities throughout your career.

Creating Personal Development Systems

Goal Setting and Tracking: Establish systems for setting, tracking, and adjusting your development goals. This might include quarterly goal reviews, monthly progress assessments, and annual planning sessions.

Feedback Collection: Build regular feedback into your routine through formal 360 reviews, informal check-ins with team members, and peer feedback exchanges with other managers.

Learning Documentation: Keep track of insights, lessons learned, and best practices you discover. This creates a personal knowledge base you can reference and share with others.

Energy Management: Understand your natural energy patterns and design your schedule to align important work with your peak performance times.

Avoiding Common Management Pitfalls

Understanding common pitfalls helps you recognize warning signs and make course corrections before they derail your effectiveness or career progression.

The Plateau Trap

Many managers plateau after achieving initial competence, becoming comfortable with their current skill level and stopping active development.

Warning Signs:

- Feeling like you've "figured out" management
- Avoiding challenging assignments or new responsibilities
- Relying on the same approaches regardless of changing circumstances
- Decreased curiosity about industry trends or best practices

Prevention Strategies:

- Regularly seek feedback about areas for improvement
- Take on stretch assignments that require new skills
- Stay curious about emerging trends and practices
- Build relationships with leaders who challenge your thinking

The Burnout Risk

Management roles involve significant emotional labor and stress, making burnout a real risk that can damage both personal well-being and professional effectiveness.

Warning Signs:

- Chronic exhaustion that doesn't improve with rest
- Decreased empathy or patience with team members
- Cynicism about organizational goals or leadership
- Physical symptoms like headaches, sleep problems, or frequent illness

Prevention Strategies:

- Set clear boundaries between work and personal time
- Delegate effectively rather than trying to do everything yourself
- Build support networks with other managers
- Invest in activities outside work that bring energy and joy

The Micromanagement Temptation

As responsibilities increase, some managers feel compelled to control more rather than delegate effectively, leading to team frustration and personal overwhelm.

Warning Signs:

- Feeling like everything depends on your direct involvement
- Team members asking permission for routine decisions
- Spending time on tasks that others could handle
- Team members showing decreased initiative or creativity

Prevention Strategies:

- Practice delegation as a skill to develop rather than a sign of giving up control
- Focus on outcomes rather than specific methods
- Invest time in developing team members' capabilities
- Regularly assess what only you can do versus what others could handle

Fatima's Long-term Development

Fatima began her management journey five years ago as a 31-year-old marketing coordinator promoted to team lead. Looking back on her growth trajectory illustrates how sustained development habits create compounding benefits over time.

Year 1: Foundation Building Fatima focused on basic management skills— conducting effective one-on-ones, giving feedback, and learning to delegate. She struggled with confidence and often second-guessed her decisions.

Year 2: Capability Expansion As her confidence grew, Fatima took on more strategic projects and began developing others. She established monthly goal reviews and quarterly development conversations with each team member.

Year 3: Strategic Contribution Fatima began contributing to organizational strategy, using data analysis skills she had developed to inform marketing investment decisions. She also started mentoring newer managers.

Year 4: Leadership Recognition Her consistent development and results led to promotion to marketing director, overseeing three teams. Fatima used her experience to create systematic development programs for other managers.

Year 5: Organizational Impact Now recognized as a high-potential leader, Fatima leads cross-functional initiatives and serves on the company's diversity and inclusion council. She's known for developing talent and has a track record of team members receiving promotions.

Key Development Habits:

- **Daily learning:** Fatima read one business article or listened to one podcast episode every day
- **Monthly reflection:** She conducted monthly reviews of her performance and set improvement goals
- **Quarterly planning:** Every quarter, she assessed her team's performance and planned development initiatives
- **Annual skill building:** Each year, she committed to developing one major new capability
- **Network building:** She consistently built relationships with peers and senior leaders

Results:

- Promoted twice in five years with significant salary increases
- Developed 12 people who received promotions or expanded responsibilities
- Led three successful product launches that exceeded revenue targets
- Recognized as "Manager of the Year" by industry association
- Built reputation as a talent developer, making her attractive to other organizations

Key Learning: Fatima's success came not from any single achievement but from the compound effect of consistent development habits maintained over time. Her investment in others also created a network of advocates and supporters throughout the organization.

Building Lasting Confidence

Management confidence develops differently than technical confidence because it involves dealing with complex human dynamics and uncertain outcomes. Building lasting confidence requires understanding what creates genuine leadership credibility.

Sources of Authentic Leadership Confidence

Competence Through Experience: Confidence grows as you accumulate successful experiences handling different leadership challenges. Each difficult conversation navigated, conflict resolved, and team goal achieved builds your belief in your capabilities.

Values Alignment: When your actions align with your core values, you feel more authentic and grounded, even in challenging situations. This authentic foundation provides stability during uncertain times.

Continuous Learning: Paradoxically, acknowledging what you don't know and committing to ongoing learning creates more sustainable confidence than pretending to have all the answers.

Relationship Quality: Strong relationships with team members, peers, and mentors provide emotional support and honest feedback that reinforce genuine strengths while identifying areas for growth.

Impact Evidence: Seeing the concrete positive effects of your leadership— team members growing, projects succeeding, problems being solved— provides objective validation of your effectiveness.

Confidence vs. Arrogance

Sustainable leadership confidence differs significantly from arrogance or overconfidence:

Confident Leaders:

- Acknowledge their limitations and seek help when needed
- Give credit to team members for successes
- Remain open to feedback and new perspectives
- Focus on serving others rather than promoting themselves
- Take responsibility for failures and learn from them

Arrogant Leaders:

- Believe they have all the answers
- Take credit for team successes
- Dismiss feedback that challenges their views
- Focus on their own advancement and recognition
- Blame others for failures

Building Team Confidence

Great leaders don't just develop their own confidence—they help build confidence in their team members:

Provide Stretch Opportunities: Give people assignments that challenge them without being overwhelming, helping them discover capabilities they didn't know they had.

Celebrate Growth: Recognize progress and effort, not just final outcomes, helping people see their development trajectory.

Share Success Stories: Tell stories about team members who overcame challenges or developed new skills, creating models of what's possible.

Support Through Failure: When people make mistakes, focus on learning and next steps rather than blame, showing that setbacks are part of growth.

Delegate Meaningfully: Give people real authority and responsibility, demonstrating your trust in their capabilities and helping them build confidence through successful execution.

Creating Long-term Impact

The most fulfilling aspect of leadership is the positive impact you can have on individuals, teams, and organizations over time. Creating lasting impact requires thinking beyond immediate results to consider how your leadership influences people's careers, capabilities, and lives.

Defining Your Leadership Legacy

Consider what you want to be remembered for as a leader. This isn't about ego or recognition—it's about clarifying the positive difference you want to make:

People Development: How many people will be better leaders, professionals, or individuals because of your influence?

Cultural Contribution: What positive changes will you make to team or organizational culture that will outlast your tenure?

Innovation and Improvement: What processes, approaches, or solutions will you develop that will continue benefiting others?

Mentorship and Knowledge Transfer: How will you share your knowledge and experience to help others avoid mistakes and accelerate their development?

Values Demonstration: How will you model principles and behaviors that inspire others to be their best selves?

The Multiplier Effect

The greatest leadership impact comes from developing other leaders who will, in turn, develop others. This multiplier effect extends your positive influence far beyond your direct reach.

Developing Your Team:

- Identify high-potential team members and invest in their leadership development
- Provide opportunities for them to lead projects and initiatives
- Share your knowledge and experience through mentoring relationships
- Advocate for their advancement and recognition

Developing Peers:

- Share best practices and lessons learned with other managers
- Collaborate on initiatives that benefit multiple teams
- Provide support and advice during their challenging periods
- Build networks that help others access opportunities and resources

Contributing to Organizational Leadership:

- Participate in leadership development programs as a mentor or facilitator
- Document and share successful approaches that others can adapt
- Contribute to succession planning and talent pipeline development
- Model the leadership behaviors you want to see throughout the organiza-

tion

David's Legacy Building

David, a 52-year-old veteran manager transitioning to senior leadership, recognized that his greatest opportunity for impact lay in developing the next generation of leaders rather than just achieving business results.

The Legacy Challenge: With 20+ years of management experience, David realized that his individual contribution was less important than his ability to multiply effectiveness through others.

Legacy Building Strategy:
Formal Mentoring Program: David established a structured mentoring program pairing experienced managers with newer leaders, providing frameworks and accountability for development relationships.

Knowledge Documentation: He created a comprehensive guide capturing lessons learned from major projects, decisions, and challenges, ensuring institutional knowledge wouldn't be lost when people moved roles.

Leadership Pipeline Development: David identified and systematically developed high-potential employees, providing stretch assignments, cross-functional exposure, and executive coaching.

Culture Change Leadership: He championed initiatives that shifted the organization toward more inclusive, collaborative leadership while maintaining performance standards.

External Industry Contribution: David began speaking at conferences and writing articles to share successful practices with the broader professional community.

Results:

- Fifteen people he mentored received promotions to senior leadership roles
- The mentoring program was adopted company-wide and became a competitive advantage for talent retention
- His knowledge documentation prevented costly mistakes during leadership transitions
- Three former mentees became mentors to others, extending the multiplier effect
- Industry recognition as a thought leader in leadership development

Key Learning: David discovered that focusing on legacy and impact created more satisfaction than any individual achievement. His shift from "What can I accomplish?" to "How can I help others accomplish great things?" transformed both his effectiveness and fulfillment.

Systems for Continuous Growth

Sustainable leadership development requires systems that support ongoing learning and adaptation throughout your career.

Personal Learning Architecture

Formal Learning: Participate in leadership programs, conferences, and courses that provide structured development opportunities.

Informal Learning: Build habits around reading, podcasts, webinars, and other resources that keep you current with trends and best practices.

Experiential Learning: Seek assignments and opportunities that stretch your capabilities and expose you to new challenges.

Social Learning: Engage with peer networks, mentoring relationships, and professional communities that provide different perspectives and insights.

Reflective Learning: Build regular reflection into your routine to extract lessons from experiences and integrate new knowledge.

Feedback and Assessment Systems

360-Degree Reviews: Conduct comprehensive feedback assessments annually to understand how your leadership is perceived by different stakeholders.

Performance Data Analysis: Regularly review metrics related to team performance, engagement, retention, and development to assess your effectiveness.

Peer Feedback Exchanges: Establish reciprocal feedback relationships with other managers who can provide honest, professional perspectives.

Upward Feedback: Create safe channels for team members to provide feedback about your leadership and areas for improvement.

Self-Assessment Practices: Develop habits of honest self-evaluation using leadership competency frameworks and personal values.

Adaptation and Evolution

Environmental Scanning: Stay aware of changes in your industry, organization, and the broader leadership landscape that might require new capabilities.

Skill Portfolio Management: Regularly assess your leadership capabilities and identify emerging skills you need to develop.

Network Evolution: Continuously expand and diversify your professional network to include people who can challenge your thinking and provide new perspectives.

Role Transition Preparation: Anticipate future career moves and begin developing capabilities you'll need for expanded responsibilities.

Legacy Planning: Consider how you want to be remembered as a leader and what steps you need to take to create that impact.

Sustaining Energy and Motivation

Leadership can be emotionally demanding, requiring strategies for maintaining energy and motivation over the long term.

Energy Management Strategies

Physical Health: Maintain exercise routines, healthy eating habits, and adequate sleep to provide the energy foundation for sustained leadership effectiveness.

Mental Stimulation: Engage in activities that challenge your thinking and creativity, preventing mental stagnation and maintaining intellectual curiosity.

Emotional Renewal: Build relationships and activities that provide emotional support and joy outside of your management responsibilities.

Spiritual/Purpose Connection: Stay connected to the deeper meaning and purpose that drew you to leadership, remembering why your work matters.

Work-Life Integration: Create boundaries and practices that allow you to be fully present in both professional and personal roles without constant stress.

Preventing Leadership Fatigue

Delegation and Development: Invest in developing others' capabilities so you're not carrying all the responsibility yourself.

Priority Management: Focus your energy on activities that only you can do while delegating or eliminating lower-value tasks.

Support Systems: Build networks of peers and mentors who understand leadership challenges and can provide advice and encouragement.

Recovery Practices: Build regular breaks and renewal activities into your schedule rather than waiting until you're exhausted.

Perspective Maintenance: Remember that setbacks and challenges are normal parts of leadership rather than signs of personal failure.

The leadership habits, learning practices, and impact focus you develop now will serve you throughout your career. The skills and perspectives you're building extend far beyond your current role, creating a foundation for leadership effectiveness that will grow and evolve as you face new challenges and opportunities.

Your commitment to sustained growth and development as a leader—evidenced by your engagement with this book and investment in your own learning—sets you apart as someone who takes leadership seriously and commits to making a positive difference through your work.

This Week's Challenge

Begin building systems for sustained leadership success:

1. **Identify three daily habits** that will support your long-term leadership effectiveness
2. **Create a personal learning plan** for the next year with specific goals and methods
3. **Establish one new relationship** with a peer or mentor who can support your development
4. **Define your leadership legacy** by writing what you want to be remembered for as a leader
5. **Set up a system** for regular reflection and self-assessment

Final Reflection Exercise

As you complete this leadership development journey, take time to reflect on your growth and commit to continued development:

Growth Assessment:

- What leadership capabilities have you developed through this book?
- Which frameworks or tools have been most valuable for your context?

186

- How has your confidence as a manager evolved?
- What impact have you already made on your team members?

Future Commitments:

- What three leadership capabilities do you want to develop further?
- How will you continue learning and growing as a leader?
- What systems will you establish to maintain your development momentum?
- How will you contribute to developing other leaders?

Legacy Vision:

- What kind of leader do you want to become?
- How do you want to be remembered by the people you lead?
- What positive difference do you want to make through your leadership?
- How will you measure the success of your leadership journey?

The journey of leadership development never truly ends, but each step forward increases your ability to create positive change, develop others, and contribute to organizations and communities that matter. Your willingness to invest in your own growth as a leader is an investment in everyone whose lives you'll touch through your leadership influence.

The foundation you've built through this book—from managing your emotional transition through strategic thinking and future-ready capabilities—positions you for continued growth and impact as a leader. Trust in your ability to learn, adapt, and make a positive difference. The world needs thoughtful, capable leaders who care about creating conditions where people can thrive.

15

Conclusion

Stepping into your first management role can feel like being handed a map in a foreign language—and expected to lead others through unfamiliar terrain. If you're reading these words, it's because you had the courage to take that first step anyway, acknowledging the nerves, doubts, and ambitions swirling inside you. This book set out to empower you—to give you not only a compass but the confidence and clarity to chart your own path as a leader who values empathy, integrity, and adaptability.

Over these chapters, you've moved from uncertainty toward assurance, gathering practical tools and mindset shifts essential for leading today's diverse workplaces. You tackled impostor syndrome by normalizing its voice and learning how to move forward despite it. You learned to build trust with small, consistent actions; to have difficult conversations that create connections rather than walls; and to foster teams where everyone feels seen, heard, and included.

The Interconnected Nature of Leadership

Every skill and insight you've developed is part of a bigger picture. From remote management strategies to inclusive hiring practices, each chapter points back to the same core truth: great leadership is built on relationships. Communication, strategic thinking, adaptability, and empathy are woven throughout everything you do—not as separate tasks, but as interconnected habits.

The emotional foundation you built in the early chapters supports every interaction you have as a leader. The self-awareness practices from Chapter 3 enable the authentic communication explored in Chapter 6. The trust-building techniques from Chapter 5 create the psychological safety necessary for the inclusive cultures described in Chapter 8. The vision creation skills from Chapter 4 connect to the strategic thinking capabilities developed in Chapter 11. Each element reinforces and strengthens the others, creating a comprehensive leadership approach that adapts to different situations while maintaining consistent principles.

This holistic approach means you're ready to face whatever challenges your team and organization might throw your way. Whether you're navigating a remote team crisis, facilitating a difficult conversation about performance, or making strategic decisions with incomplete information, you now have frameworks that help you respond thoughtfully rather than reactively.

Key Insights That Transform Leadership

Several breakthrough insights distinguish excellent leaders from merely adequate ones:

Vulnerability as Strength: Admitting what you don't know and asking for help actually increases your credibility rather than undermining it. Team members trust leaders who are honest about their limitations and committed to learning.

Empathy with Accountability: You can care deeply about your team members while still holding them to high standards. The best leaders combine genuine concern for people's well-being with clear expectations for performance and behavior.

Inclusion as Strategy: Building diverse, inclusive teams isn't just morally right—it's a competitive advantage that leads to better decision-making, innovation, and business results.

Process over Perfection: Having systematic approaches to leadership challenges (like the CALM method for conflict or the DECIDE framework for complex decisions) matters more than getting every situation exactly right the first time.

Growth over Expertise: Committing to continuous learning and development serves you better than pretending to have all the answers. The most effective leaders maintain curiosity and adaptability throughout their careers.

Your Leadership Toolkit

You now have a comprehensive toolkit that will serve you throughout your management career:

Emotional Intelligence Foundation: Self-awareness practices, emotional regulation techniques, and empathy skills that help you understand and work effectively with diverse people.

Communication Excellence: Frameworks for difficult conversations, active listening skills, and the ability to adapt your communication style to different audiences and situations.

Trust and Credibility Building: Systematic approaches to building trust through consistency, competence, and care, plus strategies for repairing trust when it's been damaged.

Team Development Capabilities: Skills for hiring inclusively, developing talent, providing effective feedback, and creating cultures where everyone can thrive.

Strategic and Systems Thinking: Ability to see the big picture, anticipate challenges and opportunities, and make decisions that serve both immediate and long-term goals.

Change and Crisis Leadership: Frameworks for leading through uncertainty, managing conflict constructively, and helping teams adapt to changing circumstances.

But even more importantly, you understand how these pieces fit together. Emotional intelligence isn't just a nice-to-have—it's the foundation for understanding yourself and the people you lead. Trust doesn't happen by accident; it's cultivated daily through honest communication and follow-through. Resilience isn't about never struggling, but knowing how to recover—both for yourself and for your team when work gets tough.

The Leadership Journey Ahead

Your development as a leader is just beginning. The frameworks and tools you've learned provide structure and guidance, but they must be adapted and refined based on your unique context, challenges, and opportunities.

Continue Learning: The leadership landscape will keep evolving. Stay curious about new research, emerging best practices, and changing workforce expectations. Build learning into your routine through reading, podcasts, courses, or conversations with mentors.

Practice Deliberately: Seek opportunities to apply these frameworks in real situations. Take on stretch assignments, volunteer for challenging projects, and put yourself in positions where you can develop new capabilities.

Build Your Network: Connect with other managers who face similar challenges. Join professional associations, attend conferences, participate in leadership development programs, or start a peer mentoring group.

Leadership is learned best in community.

Reflect Regularly: Make reflection a habit. Schedule weekly reviews of what went well and what to improve, monthly goal assessments, and quarterly strategic thinking sessions. Growth happens through experience plus reflection.

Develop Others: The ultimate test of leadership is developing other leaders. Mentor new managers, share what you've learned, and create opportunities for your team members to grow. Your legacy will be measured by the positive impact you have on others' careers and lives.

Your Leadership Legacy

Consider what you want to be remembered for as a leader. This isn't about ego or recognition—it's about clarifying the positive difference you want to make:

- How many people will be better leaders, professionals, or individuals because of your influence?
- What positive changes will you make to team or organizational culture that will outlast your tenure?
- What approaches or solutions will you develop that will continue benefiting others?
- How will you model principles and behaviors that inspire others to be their best selves?

The greatest leadership impact comes from developing other leaders who will, in turn, develop others. This multiplier effect extends your positive influence far beyond your direct reach.

A Personal Message

Your commitment to reading this book and investing in your leadership development sets you apart. Most managers learn through trial and error, often making preventable mistakes that hurt both their careers and their teams. By investing in your growth proactively, you're demonstrating the kind of thoughtful, intentional approach that distinguishes excellent leaders.

You have everything you need to succeed as a manager. You have frameworks for handling difficult situations, tools for building strong teams, and insights about what makes leadership effective. More importantly, you have the mindset and commitment to continue growing throughout your career.

The fact that you care enough about your team's success to invest in developing your leadership skills already makes you the kind of manager that people want to work for. Trust yourself, apply what you've learned, and remain open to continued growth and development.

The Ongoing Journey

Leadership is both a privilege and a responsibility. You have the opportunity to influence people's work experience, career development, and even their lives outside of work. The team members you lead will remember how you made them feel, whether you supported their growth, and if you created conditions where they could do their best work.

This responsibility might feel daunting, but it's also incredibly rewarding. There's profound satisfaction in watching someone you've mentored succeed, seeing skills you've helped develop create new opportunities for them, and knowing that your leadership has made a positive difference in people's lives.

Remember that every expert was once a beginner. The managers you most admire struggled with many of the same challenges you're facing now. They learned through experience, mistakes, feedback, and reflection—the same process you're engaged in. Your willingness to invest in developing your leadership skills already distinguishes you from managers who assume they can figure it out through trial and error alone.

The people you lead are counting on you—not to be perfect, but to be thoughtful, genuine, and committed to creating conditions where they can thrive. That's exactly what this book has equipped you to do.

Your Next Steps

1. **Choose one framework** from this book to implement immediately in your management practice
2. **Identify three leadership habits** you want to develop over the next 90 days
3. **Schedule regular reflection time** to assess your progress and adjust your approach
4. **Find one other manager** to share insights with and support each other's development
5. **Create a personal learning plan** for continued leadership growth

The journey of becoming an effective leader never truly ends, but each step forward increases your ability to create positive change, develop others, and contribute to organizations and communities that matter. Your willingness to invest in your own growth as a leader is an investment in everyone whose lives you'll touch through your leadership influence.

A Final Thought

You began this journey uncertain and perhaps overwhelmed. You're ending it with confidence, capability, and a clear sense of direction. The transformation from uncertain to confident, overwhelmed to capable, inexperienced to respected, happens through exactly the kind of intentional development work you've just completed.

Trust in your ability to learn, adapt, and make a positive difference. The world needs thoughtful, capable leaders who care about creating conditions where people can thrive. You have what it takes to be that kind of leader.

Your leadership journey is just beginning, and it's going to be extraordinary.

Welcome to leadership. Welcome to making a difference. Welcome to a career of continued growth, meaningful impact, and the deep satisfaction that comes from helping others succeed.

Thank you for allowing this book to be part of your leadership development journey. Your commitment to growing as a leader—and your willingness to invest in creating better experiences for the people you lead—gives me hope for the future of work and organizations everywhere.

Manager's Toolkit Appendix

Leadership Capability Assessment

Use this comprehensive assessment to evaluate your growth across all key management competencies. Rate yourself on a 1-5 scale (1 = Poor, 5 = Excellent) and revisit quarterly to track progress.

Trust and Credibility

- I arrive on time and follow through on commitments _____
- I demonstrate expertise while admitting knowledge gaps honestly _____
- I share reasoning behind decisions and communicate challenges openly _____
- I notice team dynamics and ask for input on decisions affecting others _____

Communication and Difficult Conversations

- I deliver clear messages that connect to team priorities _____
- I listen actively and validate others' perspectives _____
- I address conflicts directly while maintaining relationships _____
- I adapt my communication style to different team members _____

Conflict Resolution and Team Dynamics

- I recognize escalation signs and intervene appropriately _____
- I separate people from problems when mediating disputes _____
- I help teams find win-win solutions to disagreements _____
- I maintain team performance during conflicts _____

Crisis Management and Resilience

- I stay calm and make sound decisions under pressure _____
- I communicate transparently during uncertain times _____
- I provide individualized support to team members during stress _____
- I learn from setbacks and help the team grow stronger _____

Vision and Strategic Thinking

- I create compelling visions that motivate team action _____
- I communicate direction clearly across different audience types _____
- I connect daily work to larger organizational goals _____
- I anticipate challenges and adjust plans accordingly _____

Talent Development and Inclusion

- I provide meaningful feedback that drives growth _____
- I create opportunities for team members to develop skills _____
- I recognize and address bias in decision-making _____
- I foster an environment where everyone feels valued _____

Scoring Guide:

- 120-150: Strong leadership capabilities across all areas
- 90-119: Good foundation with specific areas for development
- 60-89: Developing leader with significant growth opportunities

- Below 60: Focus on fundamental skill building

* * *

Universal Conversation Framework

This modular template works for trust repair, conflict resolution, difficult feedback, and crisis communication. Adapt the elements based on your specific situation.

Preparation Phase

Clarify Purpose: What specific outcome do you want from this conversation?
Check Emotions: What emotions are you bringing? How will you manage them?
Gather Facts: What specific behaviors or incidents will you address?
Plan Approach: How will you create safety and invite collaboration?

Conversation Structure

Opening (Create Safety):

- "I want to talk about [situation] because I care about [our relationship/your success/team effectiveness]."
- "My goal is to understand your perspective and find a way forward together."

Sharing (Present Your Perspective):

- **Situation**: "Here's what I observed/experienced..."
- **Behavior**: "Specifically, what happened was..."

- **Impact**: "The effect of this was…"

Listening (Invite Their Perspective):

- "What's your take on this?"
- "Help me understand your perspective."
- "What factors should I be considering?"

Problem-Solving (Collaborate on Solutions):

- "What would need to change for this to improve?"
- "How can I better support you?"
- "What ideas do you have for moving forward?"

Closing (Make Agreements):

- "So we're agreed that you'll… and I'll… Is that right?"
- "When should we follow up on this?"
- "What support do you need from me?"

Situation-Specific Adaptations

For Trust Repair: Add explicit acknowledgment of impact and commitment to behavior change
For Conflict Mediation: Include separate listening sessions with each party before joint discussion
For Crisis Communication: Emphasize transparency about unknowns and commitment to regular updates
For Performance Issues: Include specific performance standards and improvement timeline

* * *

Weekly Leadership Practice Framework

Build consistent habits that strengthen your leadership effectiveness over time.

Daily Habits (5 minutes each)

Monday: Connection check-ins with each team member
Tuesday: Review and plan priority communications for the week
Wednesday: Practice one difficult conversation or provide meaningful feedback
Thursday: Observe team dynamics and address any emerging tensions
Friday: Reflect on leadership successes and challenges from the week

Weekly Habits (15-30 minutes each)

Team Pulse Check: How is team energy, workload, and morale?
Relationship Review: Which relationships need attention or strengthening?
Growth Planning: What leadership skill will you focus on developing this week?
Support Assessment: Which team members need additional support or recognition?

Monthly Habits (60 minutes each)

Capability Assessment: Complete relevant sections of the Leadership Assessment
Goal Alignment: Review team goals and individual development plans
360 Feedback: Seek input from team members, peers, or your manager
Learning Integration: What new approaches will you test based on recent learning?

* * *

Situational Response Guides

Conflict Response Decision Tree

Is this task conflict? (About work, goals, or procedures)
→ Yes: Facilitate discussion about different approaches and decision criteria
→ Escalating to personal conflict? Use relationship repair process

Is this process conflict? (About coordination, roles, or workflow)
→ Yes: Clarify roles and improve communication systems
→ Frequent process conflicts? Review team structure and responsibilities

Is this relationship conflict? (Personal tensions or incompatibilities)
→ Yes: Use mediation approach; separate people from positions
→ Persistent relationship issues? Consider team composition or individual development needs

* * *

Crisis Management Response Levels

Level 1 - Local Issue: Handle directly with affected team members

- Use standard difficult conversation framework
- Focus on immediate problem-solving and prevention
- Document patterns if recurring

Level 2 - Team Impact: Involve broader team in solution

- Communicate transparently about challenge and response plan
- Provide extra support to affected team members
- Monitor team morale and performance

Level 3 - Organizational Crisis: Coordinate with leadership and other departments

- Implement crisis communication protocols
- Reallocate resources as needed
- Plan for sustained response and recovery

* * *

Difficult Personality Management Strategies

Perfectionist: Set clear quality standards and revision limits; help prioritize

Pessimist: Channel critical thinking positively; balance with optimistic perspectives

Conflict Avoider: Create safe spaces for disagreement; start with low-stakes practice

Drama Creator: Don't engage with gossip; redirect energy toward problem-solving

Know-It-All: Ask for their expertise appropriately; create space for other voices

Passive-Aggressive: Address resistance directly; clarify expectations and consequences

* * *

Quick Reference Cards

Pre-Meeting Checklist

- [ ] Purpose and desired outcomes clear
- [ ] Right people included
- [ ] Materials prepared
- [ ] Time allocated appropriately
- [ ] Follow-up plan established

Decision-Making Checklist

- [ ] Problem clearly defined
- [ ] Stakeholders identified
- [ ] Options generated and evaluated
- [ ] Decision criteria clarified
- [ ] Implementation plan created
- [ ] Communication strategy planned

* * *

Team Check-In Questions

- How is everyone feeling about our current workload?
- What's working well that we should continue?
- What's one thing that would make your job easier?
- Where do you need more support or resources?
- What questions do you have about priorities or direction?

* * *

Cultural Communication Guidelines

For High-Context Team Members (many Asian, African, Latin American cultures):

- Begin with relationship acknowledgment
- Allow for indirect communication
- Provide private feedback before group discussions
- Pay attention to nonverbal cues

For Low-Context Team Members (many Western cultures):

- Be direct and specific
- Focus on facts and behaviors
- Address issues promptly
- Separate task feedback from relationship

For Hierarchical Cultures:

- Show respect for experience and seniority
- Provide clear structure and expectations
- Avoid public contradiction or correction

For Egalitarian Cultures:

- Invite equal participation
- Encourage challenges to your perspective
- Collaborate on solutions

* * *

End-of-Quarter Review Framework

Team Performance: What did we accomplish? What could we improve?

Individual Growth: How has each team member developed? What are their next growth areas?

Leadership Effectiveness: What leadership approaches worked well? What needs adjustment?

Relationship Quality: How are team relationships and communication?

Future Planning: What goals and development priorities for next quarter?

* * *

Reflection Framework

Use this approach consistently throughout the book for all reflection exercises:

Reflection Preparation

1. Find a quiet space free from distractions
2. Set aside 15-20 minutes for thoughtful consideration
3. Have a journal or notes app ready for capturing insights
4. Approach with curiosity rather than judgment

Reflection Process

1. **Read the prompt carefully** - What specific question is being asked?
2. **Consider recent examples** - What situations from your experience relate to this topic?
3. **Notice patterns** - What trends or themes emerge from your examples?
4. **Identify insights** - What new understanding or awareness develops?
5. **Plan application** - How will you use these insights in your leadership

practice?

Reflection Documentation

- Write down key insights for future reference
- Note specific actions you want to try
- Set reminders to revisit and assess progress
- Share relevant insights with mentors or peers when appropriate

* * *

This toolkit provides the foundation for effective leadership across all situations. Adapt these frameworks to your specific industry, team size, and organizational culture. The key is consistent practice and ongoing refinement based on what works in your unique context.

Manager's Resource Index

Quick Reference Guides

Framework Application Guide

- **SBI Framework**: Use for specific behavior feedback
- **CALM Framework**: Use for conflict resolution and mediation
- **GROW Model**: Use for development planning and coaching
- **DECIDE Framework**: Use for complex decisions and strategy
- **CARE Model**: Use for crisis communication
- **Trust Equation**: Use for relationship building assessment

Assessment Scale Guide

1-5 Rating Scale for All Assessments:

- **1 - Developing**: Significant growth needed, requires focused development
- **2 - Emerging**: Some capability present, needs consistent practice
- **3 - Competent**: Solid baseline capability, room for refinement
- **4 - Proficient**: Strong capability, ready for advanced development
- **5 - Exemplary**: Outstanding capability, able to mentor others

Chapter Cross-Reference Guide

- **Self-Awareness tools** → Apply in Chapters 5 (trust), 6 (communication), 10 (conflict)
- **Communication tools** → Apply in Chapters 7 (talent), 8 (culture), 12 (crisis)
- **Trust-building tools** → Apply in Chapters 8 (culture), 9 (remote), 11 (strategy)
- **Conflict resolution tools** → Apply in Chapters 7 (talent), 8 (culture), 12 (crisis)

References

Primary Research Sources

Bass, B. M., & Riggio, R. E. (2006). *Transformational leadership* (2nd ed.). Lawrence Erlbaum Associates.

Chen, S. (2023). Role transition stress and neuroplasticity in management development. *Journal of Applied Psychology*, 108(4), 623-641.

Duckworth, A. (2016). *Grit: The power of passion and perseverance*. Scribner.

Dweck, C. (2006). *Mindset: The new psychology of success*. Random House.

Edmondson, A. (2018). *The fearless organization: Creating psychological safety for learning, innovation, and growth*. Wiley.

Eurich, T. (2017). *Insight: The surprising truth about how others see us, how we see ourselves, and why the answers matter more than we think*. Crown Business.

Frankl, V. E. (1946). *Man's search for meaning*. Beacon Press.

Goleman, D. (1995). *Emotional intelligence: Why it matters more than IQ*. Bantam Books.

Grant, A. (2013). *Give and take: Why helping others drives our success*. Penguin Books.

Harvard Business Review. (2019). *HBR's 10 must reads on leadership* (with featured article "What makes an effective executive," by Peter F. Drucker). Harvard Business Review Press.

Luft, J., & Ingham, H. (1955). The Johari window: A graphic model of interpersonal awareness. *Proceedings of the Western Training Laboratory in Group Development*. UCLA.

McKinsey & Company. (2020). *Diversity wins: How inclusion matters*. McKinsey Global Institute.

Neff, K. (2011). *Self-compassion: The proven power of being kind to yourself.* William Morrow.

Page, S. E. (2007). *The difference: How the power of diversity creates better groups, firms, schools, and societies.* Princeton University Press.

Project Aristotle. (2016). *What makes a team effective?* Google re:Work.

Sinek, S. (2009). *Start with why: How great leaders inspire everyone to take action.* Portfolio.

Smart, B. D. (2012). *Topgrading: The proven hiring and promoting method that turbocharges company performance.* Portfolio.

Stone, D., Patton, B., & Heen, S. (2010). *Difficult conversations: How to discuss what matters most.* Penguin Books.

Zak, P. J. (2017). *Trust factor: The science of creating high-performance companies.* AMACOM.

Contemporary Research Studies

American Psychological Association. (2019). *Stress in America: Stress and current events.* APA Publishing.

Center for Creative Leadership. (2018). *The challenges leaders face around the world: More similar than different.* CCL Press.

Gallup, Inc. (2020). *State of the global workplace.* Gallup Press.

MIT Sloan Management Review. (2020). *Remote work productivity study: Findings from the pandemic.* MIT Press.

Stanford Work From Home Study. (2021). *The impact of remote work on productivity and career advancement.* Stanford University Press.

Management Frameworks and Models

CALM Framework for Conflict Resolution - Developed from conflict mediation research and organizational psychology principles (Center-Acknowledge-Listen-Manage).

DECIDE Framework - Classical decision-making model adapted for management contexts (Define-Evaluate-Consider-Identify-Decide-

Evaluate).

GROW Model - Established coaching framework applied to employee development planning (Goal-Reality-Options-Way Forward).

SBI Framework - Center for Creative Leadership model for effective feedback delivery (Situation-Behavior-Impact).

SMART-R Goals - Traditional SMART goals framework enhanced with Review component for ongoing assessment (Specific-Measurable-Achievable-Relevant-Time-bound-Reviewed).

Trust Equation - Mathematical framework for understanding trust components: Trust = (Credibility + Reliability + Intimacy) / Self-Orientation.

Professional Organizations and Research Institutions

Academy of Management - Professional association providing research-based management knowledge and best practices.

Association for Talent Development (ATD) - Professional organization focused on workplace learning and development.

Center for Creative Leadership - Research institution specializing in leadership development and assessment.

Harvard Business School - Academic institution contributing significant research to leadership and management theory.

Society for Human Resource Management (SHRM) - Professional organization providing research and standards for HR and management practices.

Wharton School of Business - Academic institution contributing research on organizational behavior and leadership effectiveness.

Digital and Remote Work Research

Buffer State of Remote Work Report (2023). *Annual analysis of distributed work trends and best practices.*

Microsoft Work Trend Index (2023). *Global study on hybrid work and productivity patterns.*

Remote Work Hub Research Collective (2022). *Comprehensive analysis of* *virtual team effectiveness and management strategies.*

Industry-Specific Management Studies

Healthcare Leadership Research - Studies on management effectiveness in high-stress, life-critical environments from Johns Hopkins and Mayo Clinic leadership institutes.

Manufacturing Management Best Practices - Research from MIT's Manufacturing Leadership Program on operational excellence and team leadership.

Technology Sector Leadership Analysis - Silicon Valley leadership effectiveness studies from Stanford Graduate School of Business.

Educational Leadership Research - K-12 and higher education management studies from Harvard Graduate School of Education.

Nonprofit Management Research - Leadership effectiveness studies from the Nonprofit Leadership Program at Georgetown University.

* * *

Note: This reference list includes the key sources, research studies, and frameworks referenced throughout the manuscript. Additional supporting research and contemporary examples were drawn from current business publications, academic journals, and professional development resources to ensure the content reflects current best practices and emerging trends in management and leadership. All case studies presented in the book are composite examples based on real management situations, with identifying details changed to protect privacy while maintaining educational value.